ALL HEART

ALL HEART

MY DEDICATION AND DETERMINATION TO BECOME ONE OF SOCCER'S BEST

CARLI LLOYD

WITH WAYNE COFFEY

HOUGHTON MIFFLIN HARCOURT

BOSTON   NEW YORK

hmhco.com

The text was set in Perpetua.

The Library of Congress has cataloged the hardcover edition as follows:

Library of Congress Cataloging-in-Publication Data
Names: Lloyd, Carli, 1982– author.
Title: Pure gold / by Carli Lloyd.
Description: Boston : Houghton Mifflin Harcourt, [2016] | Audience:
Ages: 10-12. | Audience: Grades: 4 to 6.
Identifiers: LCCN 2016034362| ISBN 9780544978690 (hardcover) |
ISBN 9781328695703 (e-book)
Subjects: LCSH: Lloyd, Carli, 1982—Juvenile literature. | Women
soccer players—United States--Biography—Juvenile literature.
Classification: LCC GV942.7.L59 A3 2016 | DDC 796.334092
[B]—dc23
LC record available at https://lccn.loc.gov/2016034362

ISBN: 978-0-544-97869-0 hardcover
ISBN: 978-1-328-74097-7 paperback

Manufactured in the United States of America
DOC 10 9 8 7 6 5 4 3 2 1
4500698942

To Brian, my love and husband,
and James, my trainer, friend, and mentor

CONTENTS

PROLOGUE
STARTING NOW

In 2003, I got cut from the U.S. Under-21 (U-21) team and wanted to quit competitive soccer. I was a college All-American and had made some national teams. My dream was to make the full national team. But if I couldn't make the U-21s, how was I going to make the full team? The coach who cut me told me straight out I wasn't good enough to play at the national-team level. He said I didn't work hard enough. The coach's name was Chris Petrucelli. I hated him in that moment, hated how he squashed my dream.

Now?

Now when I run into Chris Petrucelli, I tell him he's the guy who helped save my career.

For more than a decade with the U.S. Women's National Team, I've taken the field feeling as if I have to prove people wrong, starting with Chris Petrucelli.

I am one of those athletes who thrive on slights, whether

real or imagined. My trainer James Galanis calls it "the underdog mentality." He does everything he can to cultivate it. He knows I am at my best when I am playing with an edge, with some Jersey-girl attitude.

IIIII

After the first three games of the 2015 Women's World Cup in Canada, neither James nor I have to look far to find doubt-ers and doomsayers. I have come into it more fit and more ready than for any tournament I've ever played. It is my third World Cup. In the first one, in 2007, we were demolished by Brazil, 4–0, in the semifinals. In the second, in 2011, we lost to Japan on penalty kicks in the final. I was one of those who missed her PK.

Now, in 2015, it is time to change the narrative. I am a stronger, better, and mentally tougher player than I have ever been. Never mind that eleven days after the World Cup ends, I will turn thirty-three. I am so much better than I was at twenty-three. I am ready to crush it, and I believe that we, collectively, have the character and heart and skill to be the first U.S. women's team to bring home the Cup since 1999.

And then the tournament starts, and after three games, we don't look anything like the number-two-ranked team in the world. We limp out of Group D with two victories and a tie.

My confidence — soaring at the start — goes into the dumpster. I feel uninvolved, ineffective, and oddly lethargic.

The good news is that we are heading into the elimination round. The bad news for me is that my confidence is at an all-time low.

I roomed with Hope Solo, our goalkeeper, for the first two games in Winnipeg. When we checked in, there were action posters of ourselves on our beds, placed there by Dawn Scott, our fitness trainer, and other team staffers. The posters were personalized with three words.

Mine were:

Committed. Relentless. Confident.

I am a bit of a strange mix in the self-belief department. I have an almost unshakable faith in my ability to come through when it matters most and to prevail no matter what the odds. But that faith exists side by side with a stubborn, lifelong demand for perfection, and I beat myself up when I fall short. The result is that it is dangerously easy for me to hold on to mistakes, keeping them alive in an endless loop of self-criticism.

The trouble for me isn't only the expectations I have. It's

also because I tend to be super-responsible. I take things seriously. I don't want to let anybody down. When I believe I haven't played up to my standards, it's as if I'm walking around with a ball and chain.

Jill Ellis, coach of the U.S. Women's Team, meets with me before we take on Colombia in our first knockout game, in Edmonton.

"I know you are frustrated," Jill says. "But don't worry. We are going to get you going. We know what you are capable of. We know your history of coming through when the stakes are the greatest. Don't take on any huge responsibility. Don't force things. Just let it happen. You play your game, and you will be fine."

In the depths of my despair, I do what I always do in times of doubt or crisis. I reach out to James Galanis. He's on a Greek island with his family, on vacation.

"You didn't turn into a bad soccer player overnight," James says. "That is not possible. If you guys as a team were attacking and scoring goals, this wouldn't be an issue and nobody would be talking about what a disappointment the U.S. has been."

James underscores the same point Jill made: *Don't try to be perfect and change everything all at once. Don't be too fancy. Don't go for magic right out of the chute. Just go out and have fun and play. Build up slowly. Play simple balls. Connect on some passes. Get some confidence on the ball. Let yourself ease into the game, and before you know it you will be back to being Carli.*

James has one more piece of wisdom.

"When this World Cup is over, nobody is going to be talking about what happened in the group stage," he says. "They're going to be talking about the player and players who are the strongest and fittest and are powering through when everybody else is hitting their wall. They'll be talking about the players who refuse to let their team lose.

"They will be talking about you, Ms. Lloyd."

I want to believe him. I do believe him.

I get off the phone and think about how I've gotten through every other disappointment and challenge in my career: By going back to work. By working when nobody is watching, and then working some more. *You don't back off. You don't pay attention to negativity in your head. You refuse to give in.* That is what's going to set me free and get me fully engaged in this tournament.

There are, potentially, four single-elimination games left in our World Cup. I replace the loop of self-criticism in my head with something different:

It is not how you start that matters; it's how you finish.

I walk through the tunnel in Commonwealth Stadium before we take on Colombia in the round-of-sixteen, holding hands with a little kid in a bright yellow shirt and red shorts.

My World Cup starts now.

1

BEGINNINGS

FOURTEEN MILES EAST of the Liberty Bell, the small, blue-collar community of Delran, New Jersey, stretches along U.S. Route 130. It's a busy run of road with an abundance of diners, car lots and chain restaurants. Its name comes from the first three letters of DEL-aware River and RAN-cocas Creek, both of which flow through the area on their way to Delaware Bay.

My family lives in a modest neighborhood in a colonial that sits on the corner of Black Baron Drive and Parry Road. There's a side yard that is big enough to practice free kicks. There is a curb out front and two parks just down the street. I don't need a whole lot more.

My parents, Steve and Pam Lloyd, work hard to provide for my brother, my sister, and me. Dad manages his machine shop and Mom is a paralegal secretary. We are a long way from wealthy, but we have everything we need.

Limited means or not, my parents do everything they can to support all of us, especially me and my soccer. I play basketball and softball too, but from the time I start kicking a soccer ball at age five, it is my favorite thing to do.

One of the greatest thrills of my whole childhood is when my parents buy me my first pair of Copa soccer shoes. I am nine years old, and when I put them on for the first time, I feel legit, like a real soccer player.

The shoes are black leather and they are my pride and joy. I clean them after every game and practice, meticulously applying leather conditioner. I want them to stay new-looking. I want them to last forever.

I have no idea that being a professional soccer player will ever be a career option—I think it would be cool to be an FBI agent—but even as a little girl, I take soccer seriously. Nobody ever has to tell me to practice, because it is all I want to do.

The first team I play on is the Delran Dynamite. I am tiny and fast and play up front. Along with my friends Kim and Michelle, we may not quite be dynamite, but we are pretty good. Michelle's mom, Karen Thornton, is the coach, and my dad is the assistant coach. Mrs. Thornton does most of the talking and motivating. My dad is on the quiet side, which I appreciate.

Mrs. Thornton is an experienced coach who has been around sports her whole life. She teaches us and motivates us and wants us to have fun; she is positive without being smothering.

During one Dynamite game, we fall behind in the first half, and at halftime Mrs. Thornton pumps us up with her best "this moment is yours" speech. We are still behind with five minutes to play, trying our best in our gold-and-white uniforms, when Mrs. Thornton ramps up the urgency.

"Somebody's got to get one!" Mrs. Thornton yells. Kim, our goalkeeper, makes a stop and rolls the ball out. I come back and get it. I dribble past one opponent, then another. I pass midfield and get into some open space, then elude another defender. Nearing the box, I beat the last defender who has a chance to stop me and bang a shot past the goalkeeper. On the sideline, Mrs. Thornton throws up her arms and shouts her delight. I am eleven years old at the time, and beyond ecstatic. I scored a goal, and all the time and effort I'd put into practice has paid off.

I don't need a team or even a field to practice. How many times do I head out to Black Baron Drive with my soccer ball and tap the ball against the curb? A thousand? Ten thousand? I don't know. I just know it's a whole lot. I hit the ball again and again, trying to keep control even as it caroms back hard off the concrete. The cracks in the curb are my goalposts. I shoot righty. I shoot lefty. The asphalt isn't good for the cover of my ball. The repetition is very good for my ball skills.

When I need competition, I make the short trek through the neighborhood to Vermes Field. It's named for Peter Vermes, a former member of the U.S. Men's National Team who is from Delran. Or I go to the Don Deutsch Soccer Complex, named for a man who did as much as anyone to promote and grow youth soccer in Delran.

There are always boys and men from the neighborhood playing at the fields. Many of them are Turkish. I hop in and play with them all the time. I love playing free soccer. I learn to solve problems on the field, figure things out, get comfortable with the ball on my foot against good competition.

I don't know it at the time, but this is the best thing I ever could've done for my development as a soccer player. There is so much to be gained from playing this sort of soccer, unconstrained by constant whistles and coaches hollering to do this and that. A good coach is indispensable, but it's also important to be free to create and experiment.

Eventually, competition and the drive to get better help me make the difficult decision to leave the Dynamite, a town team, for a nearby club team.

Soccer starts to take over my life, in a good way. My role

model is my first cousin, Jaime Bula. She is a star soccer, basketball, and softball player who gets a college scholarship. Jaime is five years older than me. I don't have an older sister, but I don't need one with Jaime in the family. I want to be like her. I think, *If I can ever be as good an athlete as Jaime, that would be a dream come true.*

She isn't just a great athlete. She is a great person. She is as tough as she can be as a competitor, and as nice as she can be when the game is over.

In college she suffers a devastating knee injury and grinds through nine months of rehab. She makes it back for the start of the soccer season. I am in awe of Jaime's will and drive.

It teaches me a wonderful lesson: there is no substitute for hard work. Talent is great. Who doesn't want to have talent? But it's the people who work the hardest who are going to get places.

I go after things the same way Jaime does, especially in school. I am not the world's greatest student. Other kids often seem to pick things up more quickly, but I do all my work, and do it the best way I know how. The effort produces good grades, even though I remain insecure about myself as a student all the way through. When I take tests, whether multiple-choice or true/false, I doubt my answers and agonize over whether I have gotten them right.

Perfection is my goal, and that can work for you and against you. It's great to have high standards, because you don't ever get anywhere in life trying to be average or just good. On the other side, you can torment yourself along the way if you have impossibly high expectations. You can make the journey hard and joyless if you never allow yourself a few moments of contentment because you are always pushing to do even better. This is the line I walk constantly, and it's thinner than the shoelaces of my Adidas Copa cleats.

Even in soccer, as I move up in age and competition levels, there are doubts and insecurities. I make New Jersey's Olympic Development Program (ODP) team, and then the ODP Region I team, made up of the top players from thirteen states.

When I first get to the Region I camp, I size up the other players, especially the midfielders. There is Joanna Lohman, from Silver Spring, Maryland, and Sue Flamini, another Jersey girl, from the town of Cranford. They are amazing center-mids. I watch them play and think, *I will never be at their level.*

The next step after Region I is making a U.S. national team. No way can I see that happening with players such as Joanna and Sue around.

I stress about not measuring up to them. I wish that

weren't the case, but it is. I worry that I simply won't be good enough and won't keep advancing.

When the U.S. women capture the World Cup in the Rose Bowl in 1999, beating China on penalty kicks, I am totally inspired. I attend one of their games before the final and bring the team poster I have. I get autographs from Kristine Lilly, Joy Fawcett, Julie Foudy, Carla Overbeck, and others. Seeing them reach the summit of the sport ratchets up my dream even more.

Can you imagine what it would be like to play in the Olympics and win a gold medal? Can you imagine what it would be like to win a World Cup? the dream goes.

It's hard to wrap my head around what they've done, but I try. I wonder if I will ever get anywhere near such accomplishments.

You can do it if you keep getting better and work harder than everybody else, one voice inside me says.

You've got no shot. You're not even as good as Joanna Lohman and Sue Flamini, another voice says. *And what about all the other great center-mids in all the other regions around the country? Who are you kidding?*

But the first voice insists, *If you work hard and keep believing, you have a chance.*

Why are you deluding yourself? the second voice answers.

Like fencers with their swords raised, the voices keep dueling. I worry about which voice will prevail. I know which one I want to listen to. I love soccer, and I want to keep playing at the highest level I can.

I don't know what level that is, but I resolve that I will keep going for it. I am going to channel my inner Jaime and think about all she did to get back from her knee injury. I put a lot into soccer and play all the time, but I know I can do more and work harder. It occurs to me that maybe being insecure is a good thing, because it means that you will never get complacent.

Nobody understands this, or me, more than my boyfriend, Brian. Brian is two years younger, but just one grade behind me in school. He lives in the same neighborhood, just a few blocks away from Vermes Field. His best friend lives next door to my aunt Patti, so when I am over there visiting, I see him riding his dirt bike or hanging out.

We get to be good friends, united by our mutual love of sports. Brian plays on the Delran High boys' soccer team, but his best sport is golf.

Brian and I start spending more time together, and I find out from a friend of mine that he likes me. I like him, too. It's so easy to be with him. He is kind and thoughtful in a quiet, understated way. Our first night out together is a double date to see a movie. We see a horror movie. The movie scares me, but I'm happy to be with Brian.

If I am not studying or playing soccer, I am pretty much with Brian. I join his family on camping trips to Raystown Lake in Pennsylvania. In one part of the lake there are three different rock outcroppings where you can jump off into the water. The lower one is maybe a ten-foot drop. Next is probably a twenty-foot drop, and the top level must be forty or fifty feet up. It's insanely high.

I do not scare easily, and neither does Brian. I have never met a roller coaster I wouldn't go on. The hairier the ride, the more time upside down, the steeper the vertical drop, the better. Brian is the same way.

We jump off the top outcropping far over Raystown Lake, feet first. By the time I hit the water, I feel as if I am close to the speed of light.

I love it.

The time with Brian and his family is so much fun. I struggle in other parts of my life, with doubts about how I am going to measure up. I don't have to reach any standard when I am with him, don't have to be anything but myself.

2

STRIKERS FOREVER

WHEN I AM TWELVE YEARS OLD, I have what feels like a colossal setback. I have done all I can with the Delran Dynamite, and I decide to try out for the South Jersey Select team. They are the destination for all of the elite players in the area. If you are any kind of player, this is where you want to be.

I am a star player for the Dynamite, but even at this age, I know that doesn't mean too much.

I go to the Select tryout, and from the time I get out of my dad's car, the experience is daunting. I see platoons of kids milling around everywhere, more than I've ever seen at a try-out before. Almost all of them are much bigger than me. But I am used to being one of the smallest kids out there. It's never mattered before, so I try to psych myself up.

You can play with any of them, I tell myself.

I want to believe that, but do I really know? Isn't that why I am here — to see how I measure up? Tryouts are a strange phenomenon. You look around and make snap judgments about people's size, strength, character, and playing ability, all of it pretty much based on nothing. You compare yourself constantly to all of those around you:

Whoa, that girl looks tough.

Geez, that girl looks mean.

And that kid over there, wow, she looks really athletic. Can I take her 1 v. 1?

When you do something well at a tryout, you instantly look up to see if any of the evaluators noticed. If you do something poorly, you hope they missed it. It's wickedly competitive, all of us wannabe Select players going for the same blue ribbon. All of us are desperately hoping that the evaluators — these strangers with clipboards who suddenly are the most important people in your life — are favorably impressed.

Part of you wishes you could help them along:

Hey, did you see that first touch? That backheel pass? Can you tell how much it means to me to be on this team?

You want to holler all these things. You want to tell them how you don't just love soccer — you need it the same way you need oxygen. But you do not get a private audience. So you just play. You try to be at your absolute best and hope it's enough.

You do everything you can to win the blue ribbon and make the team.

The tryout ends. The list is posted. Your name is not on it. The evaluators have had a good look at everyone and decided you are not Select quality.

I do not make it.

I am devastated.

It is the first time this has happened in my years of playing soccer. I never want to show the world my emotions, and this time is no exception, but in my room it's a waterworks show beneath my Ronaldinho poster. I keep replaying the tryout in my head, wondering what I could have done differently. It's a pointless exercise, of course. It just flings open the doors to self-torture.

My parents say all the right things.

"You can learn from this and use it to make you better," my dad says. "You can turn this negative into a positive."

"This happens to everybody at some point. It isn't the end of the world, even though it might feel like it," my mom says.

I am not able to take in much of the comfort, though.

I am not sure how long I beat myself up for not making Select, but it goes on for a while. Then I get a letter in the mail. It is from a man named Joe Dadura. He is starting an Under-13 team at a club in a nearby town. It's called the Medford Strikers. He saw me at the Select tryout and thinks I am a good player. He is reaching out to other players who he believes have potential. His goal is to find enough of these players and build a team that can compete with anyone.

Soon I am wearing number 10 in the red, white, and black of the Medford Strikers. I travel three times a week to Lumberton, New Jersey, a township that was once a stop on the Underground Railroad; runaway slaves hid in the bottom of a well at a house on Creek Road.

In no time at all, I am completely sold on life as a Striker. I am part of a core of players that include Joe's daughter, Kacy; Maureen Tohidi; Venice Williams; and Quinn Sellers. They are really good players and even better teammates. We do well right off, and it all starts with Mr. D, as we call him. He's a kind, warm-hearted guy who pushes us hard and is super-competitive, but he still creates a nurturing and fun team atmosphere.

Mr. D is not a typical soccer coach in any way. He didn't grow up playing or come up through the coaching ranks; he taught himself the game by reading books, going to clinics, and watching videos. Eager to coach his three daughters, he wanted to learn enough to be able to do it. Mr. D owns a tire business, but as far as I can tell, he coaches soccer every spare second he has.

The Medford Strikers are the best team I've ever been a part of. From the back line to the front line, there are strong players all over the field. Mr. D's emphasis is on quick ball movement, clean touches, building a possession-centered attack and sound, stout defense in the back. I am in center midfield. Still a half-pint, I rely on technical skill and quick, darting runs as I probe for defensive weaknesses. I knock the ball wherever it needs to be knocked.

I want to be in the middle of everything, all the time, on the field and off. Maureen, one of my teammates, says I remind her of a gnat, flitting here and there. I jump on people's backs when they don't expect it. I sneak up from behind and try to trip them up. I steal their candy and squeeze my way onto a sofa when there is no room.

I am in constant motion, an undersized prankster on the prowl. But on the field, I am all business. I am out there to compete and to win.

We are in Florida one time for a big holiday tournament. It's raining hard and the field is a mess. Our uniforms are all white. I get pushed from behind by an opponent — no whistle — and go face first into the mud. When I get to my feet, I am covered in the stuff.

I get up and brush as much of the mud off me as I can. But I keep playing as if nothing has happened. I get my revenge where it counts the most. Seeing my opponents have to take the ball out of their net is one of the best feelings on earth.

Mr. D encourages unselfishness and team-oriented play, and it's what I love most about this team. Kacy is a really good player, a midfielder who plays alongside me. But Mr. D doesn't build the team around his daughter or around any one player. We all feel important and valued on the Medford Strikers.

There isn't any griping or sniping. Nobody acts as if she is the person who makes the whole thing go. The ball moves, and the glory is spread around. It's a beautiful thing when that happens.

We have the best time at practices and tournaments. Fun follows us around.

But Mr. D is no pushover. At one out-of-state tournament, there's a boys' hockey event going on at the same time and we are sharing a hotel with a bunch of young hockey players. Mr. D has a strict curfew of 10 p.m. before early games, but this time a teammate of mine and I decide to venture out to see where the hockey players are hanging out. It's more mischievous than anything, but when we are not back by the time Mr. D does his bed check, we are toast.

"You're sitting out the first half tomorrow," Mr. D tells me.

I know better than to try to talk him out of it, and I never blow curfew again.

Lots of times at the end of practice, I have fun without running afoul of any rules. I go to the center of the field and line up a couple of balls on the midfield line. I look toward the empty goal, about fifty yards away. I take a few steps back, sprint up to the first ball, plant my left foot beside it, and swing my right leg into it as if my leg were a sledgehammer, pounding the ball as far as I can. I do the same thing with the remaining balls, then go round them up and do it again. When I hit the ball just right, I can just about reach the goal. It's a great feeling when I do. I wonder what it would be like to try to score from there in a game.

Just as Mr. D had planned, the Medford Strikers emerge as a major player in Jersey soccer. Our core five players — Kacy, Maureen, Quinn, Venice, and me — stay together for six years. We win two consecutive New Jersey State Cup titles and soar into the national rankings. But even as we do, I struggle at times with my own expectations. I want every touch to be immaculate, every pass to be on target, every shot to find the back of the net. Of course that doesn't happen, but I am not very good at cutting myself any slack. Mistakes stay with me, gnaw on me. Maureen, our captain, has radar for it and helps snap me out of it. In one game I take a shot from distance, a good ten yards outside the 18, and miss badly. Two more shots follow, both way off target. Then both of my hands go to my head, and my head drops.

Those are the telltale signs. Maureen doesn't want to see it, or hear it.

"Forget about it. Keep plugging away. You'll get the next one," she says.

It's an on-field intervention, and I need it. Maureen has a great knack for helping me get through the thicket of self-criticism. She knows when I start to lose it almost before I do.

I am still learning to deal with adversity and not let my emotions career out of control, particularly when I am thrust into a new situation.

I make the New Jersey Olympic Development Program team in 1996, at age fourteen, all five feet, one inch, and 105 pounds of me. The way ODP works, at the end of the year, all the players in the program from the thirteen states in Region I attend a regional camp at the University of Massachusetts. The camp lasts almost a week, and at the end of it, a Region I pool team consisting of the top eighteen players is selected. Every morning during the week, a list of the players who have made the pool team for that day is posted. Then a final list is posted on the day the camp closes.

I am a mess of nerves and anxiety the whole week. For

one thing I am terribly homesick, but the bigger issue is the constant comparisons I am making. I look around and see this staggering group of talented soccer players and convince myself that I am out of my league. That this is not true is irrelevant; it's the tape that's playing in my head, and it isn't doing me any favors. In fact, it holds me back bigtime. It's hard to play freely when the gears of your brain never stop churning.

I do not make the final posted list. It's a major blow, but it teaches me an invaluable lesson about confidence. If you don't approach the game with the right mentality, you have no shot at delivering your best. I find out, as the saying goes, that "to compare is to despair." Gradually — very gradually — I learn that I am the most free, having the most fun, and playing my best when I am focused completely on my own game, not worrying about what everybody else is doing. Learning this is no different from learning how to execute a side volley or a chest trap: you have to do the training, do the reps, because it is only through rigorous training that you are going to get where you want to go. I keep working on it. It is my solution to every challenge.

3

SMACKDOWN

FOR A GUY WHOSE DAY JOB is tires, Mr. D sure gets a lot of traction out of his Medford Strikers. We become one of the top teams in the country, which gets us into high-profile tournaments, which in turn brings packs of college coaches to our tournament games, with scholarship offers in tow.

Maureen Tohidi is offered a full ride to Syracuse. Quinn Sellers accepts a scholarship from Villanova, and Venice Williams (University of South Carolina–Spartanburg) and Kacy Dadura (Niagara) do the same.

We're not the Phillies or the Eagles, but the Medford Strikers become quite a sensation in South Jersey. There are photos and glowing write-ups about us in the *Philadelphia Inquirer,* the *Burlington County Times,* and South Jersey's *Courier-Post.* Soccer fans know about us and our championship pedigree. My father is the unofficial chronicler of our acclaim, carefully cutting out all the clippings he can gather. He always brings them up to my room to make sure I know about them.

"Look what they wrote in the paper," he says. Then he takes the clips down to his desk in the garage, where he spends hours — and I mean dozens of hours over many years — arranging and pasting and putting together the most meticulous and comprehensive scrapbooks you have ever seen. My dad never wants to miss anything, and I don't think he ever has.

I have interest from dozens of colleges, an exciting if overwhelming thing to look forward to after my four years at Delran High School. I boil the competition down to two finalists: West Virginia and Rutgers. I really like the West Virginia coach, Nikki Izzo-Brown. She has built a strong program, and talking to her convinces me that she can help make me a better player and catapult me to a higher place on the national radar. That is the whole goal — to get seen by the talent evaluators at U.S. Soccer and make my way onto a national team.

Ultimately, I say no to Coach Izzo-Brown — one of the hardest things I've ever had to do — to stay in New Jersey and go to Rutgers and play for Coach Glenn Crooks.

Rutgers starts off great. I bond instantly with two of my all-time favorite teammates, Christine Wentzler and Tara Froehlich. We live together in a dormitory called Stonier

Hall, an unsightly brick box with a splendid location in the heart of campus, and we remain roommates for three years in off-campus housing. Christine, Tara, and I are inseparable, except for when they visit Rutgers's famous Grease Trucks. These are a string of lunch wagons on College Avenue that serve so-called Fat Sandwiches — sub rolls stuffed with burgers, chicken fingers, French fries, mozzarella sticks, bacon, and more — all thrown in together.

I eat one Fat Sandwich, get sick, and never have another.

The results on the soccer field are far more appetizing. We have a strong season in the Big East and get an at-large bid to the NCAA tournament, only the second in school history. We trounce Boston University in the first round and then upset number twenty-two Princeton in the second, advancing to a round-of-sixteen against perennial heavyweight North Carolina, which is 21–0 and gunning for its customary national championship.

We give Carolina its toughest game of the season, and on its home field, going up a goal in the first half before losing 2–1. We finish the season 14-8-1, and I am named All-American and Big East Rookie of the Year. I set a school record with fifteen goals and seven assists. But the bigger development for me comes when Glenn Crooks talks to Jerry Smith. Smith is the coach of Santa Clara, the reigning national champion, and the newly installed coach of the U-21 national team.

"You need to take a good look at Carli Lloyd," Crooks tells Smith. He reminds Smith how good a freshman year I had.

So Jerry Smith calls and invites me to camp. In 2002 I am in Chula Vista, California, and I am terrified. The team is loaded with big-name, bigtime players such as Aly Wagner, Nandi Pryce, and Cat Whitehill, along with a goalkeeper from the Pacific Northwest named Hope Solo. Hope is totally intimidating. She is strong and tough and has this air about her that she just might be in your face if you disagree with her about something or look at her the wrong way.

I do my best to only look at her the right way.

As scary as these players are, I caution myself to leave those feelings in the locker room. I know they won't do a thing for me on the pitch.

It works out, and I make the team.

I have a bunch of things to work on; I know that. I am not the hardest-working player in the camp. I also have defensive deficiencies, mostly because every coach I have ever had just wanted me to sit in underneath the forwards, go on the attack, and let other players worry about it when the opponent has possession. But put the ball on my foot and point me toward the attacking third and watch me go. Jerry loves that defiance, and he tells the people at U.S. Soccer that I am somebody they need to invest in.

"Carli Lloyd isn't a finished product, but she's got stuff you can't teach," Jerry tells them. "This is a player we have to develop."

The mission of the U-21 is twofold. One is to work as a feeder for the full national team. The other is to win the Nordic Cup, the biggest international tournament of the year in that age group. It is held in northern Europe every summer.

I make my first international trip for the United States, to Finland, in late July 2002. I don't get a ton of playing time, but it is exhilarating to be part of a championship effort as we knock off Germany in the final. It is a significant step up the ladder for me, and when Jerry turns the U-21s over to Chris Petrucelli, then the women's coach at the University of Texas, I expect to climb a couple of more rungs.

Except that it doesn't happen that way. In January 2003, I am coming off a second consecutive All-American year at Rutgers. But I don't seem to impress my new coach when we have the first of our monthly camps in preparation for the Nordic Cup. He is on me constantly about my defense and isn't thrilled with my fitness level either.

I don't know what this guy's problem is, I think. *Every other coach I've ever had has appreciated what I can do, and this guy only talks about what I can't do.*

We move into March and then April, and I am not sure where I stand. The fearlessness that so impressed Jerry Smith has been replaced by doubts about where I fit in with the new regime. When we do drills, I know I am as good as or better than most everyone else, and I can shoot from distance with anybody. I am scoring goals, but am I scoring any points with Chris Petrucelli?

At the close of the April camp, Chris is ready to name a roster of the players he is taking to Brazil for a pre–Nordic Cup tournament. He schedules meetings with every player. When it's my turn, we sit down in the lobby of the hotel where we are staying. People are milling about, checking in, checking out. I am oblivious to all of it. My entire focus is on my coach and the report card he is about to issue. I believe in my heart that I should go to Brazil, but I don't know what to expect.

I brace myself for Chris Petrucelli's words. He starts to talk.

"You've done okay in our camps, Carli, but the truth is that you are not performing to the level of a national team player," Chris Petrucelli says. "It's not a lack of talent; you have plenty of talent. It comes down to a lack of effort — to your tendency to take time off during the flow of play, to not doing the work we need you to do defensively.

"In my role as the U-21 coach, they want me to develop the players we have to the point where I can say, 'I recommend this player for the national team.' And the simple fact is that you have not put yourself in a position where I can say that."

Chris Petrucelli finishes by telling me that I will not be making the trip to Brazil, or to the Nordic Cup.

He stands up to signal the meeting is complete. I stand up too. I remember nothing else. I am in a daze. It is by far the most stinging evaluation I have ever received in my soccer career.

I manage to avoid breaking down in front of him — I am not sure how — and slowly walk away. I honestly don't recall uttering an insincere "Thank you," or wishing him a great day, or saying anything at all; I am so numb from this face-slap that I can't even think.

I get back to my room and call my parents. They can barely hear me between the sobs.

"Chris Petrucelli just cut me from the U-21s. He says I'm not a national-team player," I tell them.

My parents do their best to comfort me, they really do, but I can't take any of it in.

"I don't know if I want to keep doing this national team thing," I tell them. "It's not going anywhere. The players here are so good. The coach just finished telling me I'm not at that level. Maybe it's time to come home and just play out my final year at Rutgers and be done with it."

I fly home to New Jersey. I am sure I will never wear a USA jersey again.

|||||

Chris Petrucelli's rebuke is still burned into my psyche days before the U-21 team is set to leave for Denmark and the 2003 Nordic Cup. It feels awful to think a year ago I went to Finland with Jerry Smith's team and now here I am lying in my bedroom in Delran, looking at my Ronaldinho poster and wondering how things got so fouled up. I haven't been with the U-21s for a couple of months. I have no idea what my soccer future is. I am at a crossroads, a midfielder in a muddle. The more I think about it, the more I am convinced that it is time to give up the chase. As I told my parents, I will play my senior year at Rutgers, get a degree, and try to find a job. What's the point in putting in all the work on the field when clearly U.S. Soccer doesn't think I'm good enough?

If I can't stick with the U-21 team, how am I ever going to

make the full national team? This is my belief, and don't try to talk me out of it. You've got no shot.

As I try to sort it all out, I find out that the U-21s are looking for a friendly game before they leave. They have made arrangements to play a top Jersey club team that I sometimes play for. I am going to get to play against the coach who just told me I wasn't national team material.

Do payback opportunities get any better?

I figure I am on my way out of the U.S. Soccer orbit, but I don't mind leaving behind a few reminders of what might've been.

I don't have anything personal against Chris Petrucelli. I just want to show him that there's more to my game than he thinks. I don't work hard? I can't defend? I'm not national-team-worthy? We'll see about that.

I am all over the place in the friendly against my former team. I win fifty-fifty balls. I tackle hard. I go on the attack and generate threats. I don't remember the score, but I do remember that I bring it the whole game.

The next day, I get a call from the man who ripped my heart out, Chris Petrucelli. Kelly Wilson, an All-American forward for the University of Texas who had already played, and scored, for the full U.S. Women's National Team, suffered an injury in the friendly and won't be able to compete in the Nordic Cup.

"We need another player. Would you like to take the spot?" Chris asks.

"Yes, thank you," I say. "When do we leave?"

|||||

In the opening game against host Denmark, in the medieval city of Randers, Chris calls for me in the eightieth minute with the game still scoreless. We have been dominating, but the Danish goalie, Heidi Johansen, keeps coming up with huge saves. She is the keeper on the full Danish national team, and it isn't hard to see why. We end the game with twenty-five shots, Denmark with three. The trouble is, we are not finishing them. The scoreboard says the game is tied, and that is all that matters.

"If you get a chance, go ahead and knock one," Chris says to me.

Almost instantly, I get a chance. I carve out enough space to drive a shot from the top of the box. Johansen knocks it down, and my teammate Lindsay Tarpley pounces on the rebound but knocks it just wide.

We keep pushing the attack. Seven minutes later, I beat a Danish defender and pound another shot, this time from twenty-five yards out. Johansen tracks it well, but the ball has too much pace to catch, so she deflects it away. Tarpley, again, is on the doorstep, picks up the rebound, and buries it. In just seven minutes, I have contributed two big scoring chances, the second of them an assist on the game-winner. It is something to build on, I hope.

We go on to beat Iceland, tie Norway, and come from behind on two goals by Joanna Lohman, our captain, to beat Sweden for our sixth Nordic Cup title in seven years. I am thrilled to be on the winning side, but frustrated that I played a total of only sixty-five minutes in the tournament. Being a late injury replacement, realistically I could not have expected more, but I head home full of more doubts than ever about where this is going. I am twenty-one years old. I am no better than a fringe member of the U-21 team, even though I've just been part of another Nordic Cup championship.

That is the truth. Why pretend otherwise?

I spend the rest of the summer training with the Philadelphia Charge of the Women's United Soccer Association (WUSA), thinking that this could be an option after I graduate.

I love to play soccer, and if the U.S. national team doesn't want me, maybe I will just play pro soccer, I think.

Then, in September, the entire league folds.

It feels as if doors are closing all over the place, and then things get even worse. Brian and I are out one night when he tells me, "I think we should stop seeing each other for a while."

My insides instantly go cold and numb. I briefly consider the idea that he might be kidding, but then I look into his eyes and realize that he is not kidding at all.

I am beyond shocked.

"Why do you say that?" I say.

"I don't know, I just think we need some space. You have a lot going on, and so do I. Things haven't been the same lately. It's just a gut feeling I have."

Brian and I had a breakup a few years before, just as I was starting at Rutgers. I was starting to travel a lot, and when summer came around, he wanted to be with his friends. But I never doubted we'd wind up back together. This time he catches me much more off guard.

"Well, okay, if that's what you want, fine," I tell him.

I try to be brave, but I want no part of a separation, or space. I have no choice but to go along and trust that things are going to work out.

Brian and I stay in touch periodically, and I have a good year for Rutgers. We make it back into the NCAA tournament, drawing Maryland in the first round. I score on a one-timer in the first half, before the game ends in a 1–1 tie and we wind up winning on PKs.

Next up is Penn State, ranked number six in the country, a team anchored by Joanna Lohman, Nordic Cup teammate turned NCAA opponent. Joanna is such a good player, and a ferocious worker. She just goes and goes, and her level of play is as consistent as a metronome. I really admire that about her.

Joanna scores early, and Penn State goes up two goals in the first six minutes. I blast a ball into the upper corner in the fourteenth minute, but we can never quite catch up. Then Joanna scores again in the eighty-fifth minute to make it 3–1. Our tournament, and season, are over, and my soccer soul-searching commences anew.

Three years into my Rutgers career, I've scored and assisted on lots of goals, won a bunch of honors, and helped turn us into a winning program. I am often mentioned in conversations about the top collegiate players in the country. Yet I still feel strangely unfulfilled.

I still feel like an underachiever.

People have been telling me for years that I am going to wear a USA jersey someday, so how come I am going backwards? Were they just saying that to be nice?

Are Chris Petrucelli's words ("not performing to the level of a national-team player") going to be my soccer epitaph?

Not long after my college season ends, I get a call from my father. He has just had an impromptu meeting with James Galanis of Universal Soccer Academy in the parking lot off of Ark Road in Lumberton. It was raining hard. James was packing soccer gear into his car, eager to get dry and get home. My father approached him and asked if he had a minute.

"I don't know if you remember, but you saw my daughter, Carli Lloyd, a couple of years ago when you were training one of her Medford Strikers teammates," my father said. "She's been on the U-21 national team and is looking to get back into the national program. Would you be willing to meet with her and, if you think it's a good fit, train her?"

James thought for a moment.

"I remember your daughter," James told my father. "If she is interested, tell her to give me a call."

"Thank you," my father replied. "I will do that. I am sure she will be reaching out to you soon."

My father calls to share the news. I hear the excitement in his voice. He is convinced James Galanis can make a difference for me.

"He's an excellent trainer. I think you should at least talk to him and see what your take is," my father says. "It can't hurt, can it?"

"I'll think about it," I tell my father.

And I do think about it. A week passes. Another week passes. Thanksgiving comes and goes. I am still thinking. I'm not quite sure what my resistance is, but I am a little skeptical and a lot guarded. What are the chances that this guy is going to tell me something I haven't heard a hundred times before?

Why should I take the time to meet with a trainer who, however much he might know, is not working anywhere near the national team level? My honest feeling is that nothing is going to help at this point.

Finally, in early December, I call this James Galanis. He has such a thick Australian accent that I can barely understand him. I am standing up and pacing around my bedroom with the door closed, anxious to get the call over with. He asks me a few questions about my college season and my history with the U-21s. We set up a time to meet when I am home for winter break.

A few weeks later, on a Thursday night, I pull into the lot on Ark Road in my little black Saturn. It's after eight o'clock. The temporary light stanchions cast a faint glow on the frozen field. James has set up rows of sticks and cones. This is his first up-close look at me in several years.

"What do you say we start with some skill work and see where we are?" James says.

"Sure," I reply.

For the next hour, I audition for James Galanis. I juggle. I dribble in and out of the poles. I demonstrate my first touch, passing, volleying, my technique on the ball with every part of both feet.

In between drills, James asks questions.

"Why do you think you were cut from the U-21s?"

"I don't know. I don't think I was the coach's type of player," I say. "He didn't seem to like me."

"What sort of teammate are you? Do you connect with people and support others?" he asks.

"That wasn't easy on this team. The team was full of cliques. It was hard to get any chemistry going. I don't think I really had a chance to show them the type of player I am."

"Do you like to go on the attack?" James asks.

"Yeah, I do. I like to take people on and send through balls, and I have a strong shot."

"Do you get back on defense at all?"

"No, I don't do that much. I just sit behind the strikers."

"Why?"

"That's what I'm best at. That's what my coaches want me to do," I say.

Almost every answer I give James is full of excuses. The amount of ownership I take is nearly none.

The session lasts an hour. I am gassed about twenty minutes into it. I don't mind all the questions because it gives me time to rest. When we're done, James says he wants to meet again on Saturday to do a fitness evaluation.

"This wasn't fitness, what we did tonight?" I ask.

"No, this was just an evaluation of your skill," he says.

I don't say anything. All I can think about is what a mess I will be at the end of a fitness evaluation if I feel this way after only working on skills. Still, there is something I like about James. He is very clear and direct. I like the questions he asks and the way he asks them. I like that he doesn't baby me. He hasn't talked about setting any standards or goals yet, but I can tell his are very high.

I report to our designated meeting place, on the track at Lenape High School in Medford, New Jersey, on Saturday afternoon. James says he wants me to do the Cooper Fitness Test, running at a steady pace for as far as I can go over twelve minutes.

"Without stopping?" I ask.

"Yes, without stopping," he says.

After a brief warm-up, I am ready. Off I go around the track, one lap and another and another. I want to stop, but I don't. I think I might throw up at one point, but I don't do that, either. I finally finish up. Eight laps — two miles — is considered excellent. I don't even get to five — a mile and a quarter. All-American midfielder? Ha.

I look over at James, and he is not saying anything or betraying any emotion. His silence is making me nervous.

Next I have to do interval work, running 400 meters, then 200 meters and 100 meters. I go hard and do my best, but honestly, it's not very good and I know it. During the rest intervals, James asks more questions.

What's up with all these questions? I think.

When all the track work is done, I knock out as many sit-ups and push-ups as possible in two minutes. And then James asks me to sit down on the red bleachers. It's just the two of us at an otherwise deserted track. I feel as if I'm about to have the biggest exam of my life, and I hope I don't mess it up.

"So tell me, what do you want to do with your soccer career?" he asks.

"I want to play for the U.S. Women's National Team," I say.

James is quiet for a few moments. The quiet stokes more anxiety. Part of me wonders if he is going to laugh, or tell me that I am in fantasyland.

Finally, James speaks.

"Okay, this is the story as I see it," he says. "Can you do

it—make the U.S. Women's National Team? Yes, you can do it.

"Is it going to take a lot of work? It is going to take a whole lot of work. A whole lot. But if you put in that work, then I don't see any reason why you can't go as far as you want to go."

I take in his words. I look up and down the red grandstand and then at this young Aussie guy a few feet away, with long dark hair and the thick-legged, athletic physique of a soccer player. I know very little about him, truthfully. But as I sit and listen to him, I have complete trust in what he is saying. I'm not sure I can even tell you why. He seems smart and very knowledgeable about the game, but more than that, he seems real. Usually it takes some time before I am ready to let my guard down around people I don't know well, but with James it happens almost instantly. I am encouraged for the first time in a long while. I want to hear more, and James obliges, providing the most detailed evaluation of me as a player that I've ever gotten.

It begins with him telling me about the Five Pillars, which he sees as the essential components of any world-class player.

"The Five Pillars are technical skill, tactical awareness, physical power, mental toughness, and character," James says. "To be an elite player you need to have them all. From what I see after this evaluation, you are strong in the first two. You are good on the ball, very comfortable on the ball. That's vitally important, because not many players have that. You also show a keen tactical awareness, and that's important as well.

"But the other three? Those are areas where you are sorely lacking. You are not fit, and that's going to be a big challenge, because fitness does not come naturally to you. Mentally, you are weak. You don't push yourself hard and you are lazy, and you aren't the sort of player who is going to thrive under pressure. And your character? That is poor. You make excuses and find people to blame and don't want to look at your own role in things. You always have a reason why things are not working out, instead of focusing on what you can do to make them work out."

James Galanis has pretty much just shredded me, and I am fine with it. I am not defensive at all, because I know he is 100 percent right. I don't argue or push back on anything he is saying. It is almost as if I'd been waiting for someone like him my whole life.

He continues.

"If you keep working at eighty percent, you won't get anywhere," he says. "You need to stop with the excuses and blaming this person, that person, and the man in the moon. You need to start treating every training session, every game, as if it were a World Cup final. You need to be the hardest-working person out there, every time, no exceptions. You can't just sit behind the strikers and feed them through balls and be a one-way player. You need to play box-to-box. You need to defend and do the dirty work. You complain about the coach not giving you enough time? You need to give the coach no choice but to give you time. That is what it will take, Carli.

"So here's the deal: soccer needs to be number one in your life. Not your boyfriend or your social life or anything else. Soccer. That's what it will take. If it's not number one, let's go home right now, because it won't work and we will be wasting our time. If I call you at 10 p.m. on a Saturday night and say, 'Meet me at the field in a half-hour,' I don't want to hear, 'Sorry, Coach, I'm at a party or I am out with friends. Can we get together tomorrow?' No, I want to hear, 'Okay, I will see you there.' You have to be ready and willing to train on Christmas and Easter and Thanksgiving, and all the other days that other people are resting. That's what kind of commitment it's going to take. If you are willing to make it, I will be happy to work with you. I will do everything I can to help you reach your goals, because I know you have a lot of ability and I believe you have greatness in you. It is up to you. We have to build this foundation, day by day. We have to build on the strengths you have and get to work on the things you don't have. If you're ready, then let's get to work."

My head is spinning, but it's spinning in a good way.

"When do we start?" I ask James Galanis.

Climbing into my black Saturn, I feel as though I've just gotten an infusion of hope. Everything is looking up. It's not just the prospect of working with James. Brian and I bump into each other at a party, and we talk for a while. It's natural and easy. We reconnect, and soon we are back together. I was sure that would happen, but it's an immense relief now that it has. With Brian is where I want to be, where I always want to be. I share with him the news about James and what a difference I think he can make.

"You only get one shot at this. I'm glad you are going for it," Brian says.

4

NATIONAL ATTENTION

I DON'T KNOW IT at the time, but James Galanis and I have much in common. As a player, he was a tough-tackling midfielder who could score from distance. He could slice balls all over and change fields with a fifty-yard crossfield ping. And like me, he grew up in a working family that knew nothing about privilege or abundance.

James's parents come from a region in Greece called Symou, and neither of them had it easy. His father was the oldest of seven children, and dropped out of school in fifth grade to help his father—James's grandfather—run a small general store on a mountaintop. James's mother dropped out a year earlier, in fourth grade, to work in the tobacco fields. James's parents emigrated to Australia to get a fresh start. His father was eighteen years old when he left his homeland; his mother sixteen. They lived only ten kilometers apart in Greece, but never met until they both arrived in Melbourne. There, they fell in love, got married, and raised a family in a little hard-scrabble town called Preston.

James was the middle child of three, and the language spoken at home was Greek. James didn't speak any English when he started school, which made for a miserable experience. Other kids teased him. The teachers thought he was dumb because he couldn't understand English. James couldn't stand school and hated the way it made him feel. The only thing that saved him was soccer. James started playing at an early age. He picked it up quickly, and when he got a little older, his soccer skills made him popular. Suddenly he wasn't the dumb Greek kid anymore; he was the kid you wanted to have on your soccer team.

James had two idols as a youngster. One was Diego Maradona, and the other was Bruce Lee. James was fascinated by the martial arts. When he discovered there was a top karate school, named Goju Ryu, right near his house, he would go there and sit on the steps outside and watch. One day when he was about eleven, someone invited him in and introduced him to an instructor.

"If you like karate so much, why don't you just join the club?" the instructor asked.

"My parents can't afford it," James said.

"Mate, tell your parents if they pay sixteen dollars for a uniform, you can train for free," the instructor said.

James got his uniform, and from then on, if he wasn't on the soccer field, he was in karate class. He worked his way up through the ranks — white, yellow, green — until he finally made it to black belt. At age fifteen, his instructor entered him in a tournament. James had no idea what was at stake, or who he would be competing against. He showed up and won his first fight, and then his second and his third, and wound up making it to the state championship.

James's karate training taught him about discipline, hard work, and the importance of technique — breaking skills down to specific components, all of which must be executed flawlessly. It also taught him about the power of the mind, as he learned to meditate and visualize what he wanted to do in his bouts.

The rigors of his karate training helped James's soccer. He began playing with a local adult team at age fifteen, before signing to play professionally with a club called Clifton Hill. He dropped out of high school at sixteen to play soccer, over his parents' vehement objections.

James studied to be an electrician's apprentice, but mostly he played soccer, earning a reputation as one of the premier players in the area.

Eventually, James moved to the U.S. and settled in South Jersey. There he started coaching soccer and launched his own business, Universal Soccer Academy.

IIIII

I am not James's only soccer pupil, but I quickly become a regular. I start training with him almost immediately after the evaluation. Soon after, he maps out a three-phase master plan for me. Phase I (2004–2008) is getting me well entrenched with the U-21s and into the mix with the full national team. Phase II (2008–2012) is continuing to improve my fitness and sharpen my overall game and solidify my standing on the U.S. Women's National Team. Phase III (2012–2016) is to become a dominant player for the U.S. — and the best player in the world.

It is good he doesn't share this with me, because it might make my head explode. You don't start fixating on the finish line of a marathon when you're steps into the first mile.

Suddenly, the entire focus of my soccer life has shifted. I am training with James four or five times a week, often two sessions of three hours apiece.

Once I am back in school at Rutgers, I make the 100-mile round trip down to South Jersey more times than I can count.

James says soccer has to come first, and he isn't kidding. If

I am not actually working out with James, I am texting with him or talking to him about our workouts, or I am off doing fitness work.

That typically happens at Laurel Acres Park, which has a stocked fishing lake, picnic grills, and five ball fields. I am not there to have fun. I am there to punish my body into shape. I do repeat sprints up the big hill that is Mount Laurel's top sledding location. I run the hill forwards and backwards and do occasional suicides. It is a killer supplement to the distance running I do on the streets. James wants me to be able to run ninety minutes. That is what I am pushing for, and to get there, I am going hard, all the time.

I am invited to Chris Petrucelli's U-21 camp in 2004. Right from the start, I am a different player. I am not a pretender anymore. I am not even just a contender. At each monthly camp we have leading up to the Nordic Cup, I am emerging as a leader, even in the eyes of the coach who stomped on my dream about nine months earlier.

In late March we embark on a trip to China to play three games in the greater Shanghai area. It is the first of my many trips to China, and it is a body-clock shock, a culture shock, a diet shock. Honestly, if I had gone to Mars, I don't think it would've been as much of a jolt. I am so amped up I can't even sleep on the flight over, so I binge-watch movie after movie after movie on my portable DVD player. I am seriously jet-lagged when we land in Shanghai, and that only heightens the sensory bombardment. I am not even close to being in my comfort zone, but thankfully the soccer part of the trip is much more agreeable.

I score a goal in a 4–0 victory over a top club team in the first game, and then we travel to the city of Jiangsu, not far from the Yangtze River, to play the Chinese women's national team. When we walk out, I am stunned by the sight before me. About ten thousand people are in the stands, nearly all of them wearing black or gray clothing. It is by far the biggest crowd I've ever played in front of. It makes me nervous. I keep looking up at all these people, a monochromatic sea of fans who are mostly quiet and polite. I can't fathom that they are all there to see us play. The fans in Jiangsu do not get a whole lot to cheer about. I open the scoring in the eighteenth minute, and then feed our striker, Natasha Kai, who scores another goal two minutes later.

We win all three games and return home. I'm happy with how things go and delighted not to look at a cut of meat and wonder if it's a dog.

We continue with our monthly camps in preparation for the Nordic Cup in July. When I am not there, I am working faithfully with James, who more and more is drilling me on the psychological piece of this. It is so easy for me to lose faith and doubt myself. Being aware of such tendencies is the first defense to reining them in. James helps me see that I don't have to listen to those self-critical and negative tapes that might be playing in my head. I have a choice.

It's hard to break an engrained habit, but being able to recognize it helps. In one camp session, I struggle with my first touches and get stripped a few times. I don't have the right weight on several passes, resulting in giveaways. Right away my head starts spinning and the doubts fire up. I am disgusted that I am not playing well.

The minute I realize what I'm doing, I remind myself what James has taught me:

Just because you might have those thoughts doesn't mean you have to pay attention to them.

Just because you have them doesn't mean they are true.

|||||

In our April camp, I get a chance to play with some national-team players. At the end of the month, my phone rings. It is April Heinrichs, coach of the U.S. Women's National Team.

"The whole national team staff, along with Chris [Petru-celli] and his staff, have been very impressed with your ability and your potential to grow as a player at this level," April says.

"We'd like to invite you to train with the full national team next month in Carson, California."

I am not expecting this. I am so thrilled I have a hard time finding the words, before stammering out a few.

"Thank you so much, Coach. It will be an honor to be there."

I have final exams coming up at Rutgers, but as much as I know it's important to get my degree, my entire focus is on Carson. When I walk out on the field for the first time, I know I will look around and see players such as Mia Hamm, Kristine Lilly, Briana Scurry, Julie Foudy, and Joy Fawcett. I know I will be as nervous as I've ever been in my life.

Calm down, Carli. They are soccer players, the same as you, I tell myself.

It doesn't work.

I mean, these are legends of the sport. I have their posters and autographs. I don't know what to call them or how to interact with them. Do I walk up to Mia Hamm and say, "It's an honor to be on the field with you"? Am I supposed to act as if I am a peer? I don't know. April Heinrichs is super-nice and welcoming. I hope the players are the same way.

|||||

When I arrive in Carson, two of the first people I meet are

Shannon MacMillan and Tiffeny Milbrett, both very gifted forwards. They could not be nicer.

"It's great to meet you and have you in camp," Shannon says. "I remember when I came into my first camp. It's not easy, but once you settle in and play your game, you will be fine."

Tiffeny is the same way. She greets me warmly and seems genuine. "Let me know if you need anything," she says. I find out quickly that Shannon and Tiffeny are more the exception than the rule, because from the outset most everybody else is somewhere between aloof and downright chilly.

I am reserved to begin with, not someone inclined to be chatty in new situations, but the atmosphere makes me even more of a loner. Almost nobody introduces herself. I'm not expecting a basket of fruit, but I barely even get acknowledged. I get the feeling that they would much prefer it if I were not there. Heather Mitts, a friend and longtime national team defender, tells me later she had the same experience when she first came on. So does Danielle Fotopoulos, a reserve on the 1999 World Cup championship team and another player in the 2004 camp who goes out of her way to make me feel a part of things.

"Don't take it personally, because it's not about you in the least," Danielle says, before sharing a story about her own early years, when she was sitting in the locker room, not far from a veteran team member who did her best to ignore Danielle. A few other newcomers came in, and the vet still wasn't talking. Then another longtime player showed up, and the veteran suddenly turned into Ms. Sociable.

"Finally, somebody who I actually care about," the veteran player said.

When I hear this story, I make a promise to myself: If I ever make this team, I am not going to freeze out the young players this way. I am going to treat people with civility, the way they should be treated—even someone who plays my position.

It's not only the nice thing to do. It's the right thing to do.

It feels as if it's a girls' club, and new members are not exactly welcome.

It's a strange dynamic when you get to the national team level, and it's probably this way in every sport. There are very few spots on the team, and the competition to get them is wicked. Anyone new is viewed, to some degree, as the enemy. I wish it were not that way.

April is extremely positive and encouraging to me, praising my technical skills and first touches. That seems to make me even more disliked by the veteran players. I do my best to put it all out of my mind and play, but it isn't easy. The pace of play is so fast — faster than any field I've ever been on. All around me are world-class athletes who are on you in a second, primed to pounce on every loose touch. I feel as though I am barely able to keep up.

One day we are playing 5 v. 5, and I am on Briana Scurry's team.

"You've got to do better than that," she snaps when somebody gets around me.

I get a glare and another dressing-down from Mia Hamm, who doesn't like the pace and location of a pass I make to her.

"C'mon! That's not a ball I can do anything with!" she says.

I know I'm on the field with the best players I've ever played with, and it's going to be an adjustment. Nerves aren't helping. I do my best to let the criticisms come and go.

Remember what James said, I tell myself. *Be the hardest-working player out there. Leave it all on the field. Every practice is a World Cup final.*

I work hard and take chances. I shoot from distance whenever I have an opening. Even when I am nervous and insecure, I always have confidence in my ball-striking. It is my calling card. Early in camp, I rip a shot from thirty yards out that sails high but has a lot of pace on it.

"Wow," I hear a couple of the veterans say. April notices too.

I don't make the eighteen-player roster for the Athens Olympic Games later that summer, but I never really expect to. (April tells me much later that I was one of the final cuts and that if I'd been in camp a little longer, I would've made it.) So I shift my focus to another Nordic Cup for our U-21 team. This time it's being held in Iceland, where the water smells like sulfur, the scenery and hot springs are divine, and it almost never gets dark, at least not in July.

We cruise through the tournament again, beating all four opponents by the same 3–0 score. I score from distance to finish off Germany and put us in the final. Then we crush Sweden for the championship.

The much bigger women's soccer tournament of the summer, though, takes place in Athens. The U.S. wins the gold medal on a diving header in overtime by Abby Wambach, a 2–1 victory over Brazil; it is the final international game that Mia Hamm, Kristine Lilly, Julie Foudy, Brandi Chastain, and Joy Fawcett will ever play together. It's truly the end of an era. Twenty-four-year-old Abby is figured by many people to be the team's next breakout star, the player who will keep the U.S. on top.

I am six months into my work with James, and despite how much progress I've made in that time, I am impatient that it hasn't happened faster. Lindsay Tarpley is a twenty-year-old hybrid forward/midfielder and a rising star who scored the first goal in the final in the Olympics. Twenty-two-year-old Aly Wagner has been a U.S. soccer golden girl since she was a teenager. She's considered the attacking midfielder of the future, and she's another 2004 Olympian.

Where does this leave me? Why does there have to be a talent clog in the exact position that I play?

Later, at national team camp, I am sitting alongside Danielle Fotopoulos in a van on our way to training.

"I've been working so hard for the last five or six months to get ready for this," I say. "I feel like I'm not even getting a look. Sometimes I don't feel like I'm getting anywhere."

Danielle looks at me like a kindly older sister.

"You have to try to be patient, Car," Danielle says. "Five or six months is just warming up. It is nothing in the big picture of things. This is hard, and you can't forget that. It doesn't happen all at once, and you can't expect it to and can't let yourself get frustrated by that.

"It just takes time. Even Mia Hamm was a backup for a number of years. You just have to make up your mind that you are going to outlast everybody else, and then you will be exactly where you want to be."

I think about Danielle's choice of words . . . *outlast everybody.*

I like the way they sound.

5

ONE CAP AT A TIME

It's an idyllic summer Sunday in Portland, Oregon, six days before my twenty-third birthday, in one of the prettiest soccer settings in the United States. The date is July 10, 2005. The U.S. Women's National Team is about to take on the Ukraine at Merlo Field on the campus of the University of Portland. The day's dominant story line centers on Tiffeny Milbrett, a hometown girl who starred at Portland before going on to a superb career as a high-scoring forward for the national team. Tiffeny is one goal shy of one hundred for her career, and what would be better than for her to reach the milestone here at home?

Everybody hopes Tiff gets it done, though the truth is that I am preoccupied with my own milestone, albeit a much humbler one. Several days earlier, at the end of a training session at a national team camp, Greg Ryan, who had just replaced

April as the national team coach a few months earlier, gathered everyone together.

"It's been a good camp. Thank you all for your hard work," he said. "Okay, this is the roster we're going to go with for the Ukraine match."

I felt as if I'd had a good camp, but I'd already learned you take nothing for granted when it comes to the national team, whether it's being invited to camp or making a roster cut. I've gotten really good news from coaches, such as when April invited me to my first full national team camp fourteen months earlier. I've also gotten really bad news, such as when Chris Petrucelli sent me home from the U-21s.

Greg started to read the list. I could barely stand the anticipation. Greg began with the team captain, Kristine Lilly.

He went on, running through a familiar group of names, in alphabetical order: Fotopoulos . . . Markgraf . . . Milbrett . . . O'Reilly . . . Tarpley . . . Wagner . . . Welsh.

Somewhere in the middle he said:

"Lloyd."

Did I hear that right? Lloyd?

Did Greg Ryan just announce my name?

Yes, he did.

Truly, he did.

I looked around the field, and it was almost as if a tidal

wave of euphoria was going to sweep me away. How often in life do you think and dream about something for so long — in this case, more than half my life — and then have it come true?

I had made it onto the U.S. Women's National Team. I was not just in the camp, not someone they were just checking out. I was on the roster.

I was in disbelief.

I couldn't wait to share the news with James. I couldn't wait to tell Brian and my parents.

The equipment manager came over and told me I needed to pick out a uniform number. I was given the available options and decided on 22, the number my cousin Jaime used to wear.

I don't wear Jaime's old clothes anymore, but I still want to be like her.

The night before the game, I was a nervous wreck. I wondered if I was even going to be able to play. Would I trip on a shoelace running out for warm-ups? Would I be able to make a touch without knocking it halfway to the moon? I called James for reassurance; I knew he would say the exact right thing, because he always does. We'd been working together eighteen months, and he knew me better than I do.

"It's the same game and you are the same player," James

said. "Think of all the training we've done to get to this point. I guarantee nobody on the team has put in greater effort or commitment to get to this position.

"Don't overthink it. Just go out and play. Let your training do the talking. If the coach calls for you, keep it simple in the beginning and take more and more risks as things go on. No matter what, be the hardest-working player on the field and walk off knowing that you emptied the tank."

Before we hung up, James had a few final words.

"Whether you play the full ninety or you don't play at all, I am proud of you — as a student and as a person. Remember, this is just the starting point. We are going to keep working, and you are going to get better and better and better."

James' words were a big comfort, but I still had a restless night and couldn't stop thinking about what it would be like to put my kit on and see the 22 jersey with the name LLOYD on top of it. My friends Nandi Pryce and Danielle Fotopoulos took turns trying to calm me down. In the pregame, I felt completely gassed just doing basic warm-up drills, my adrenaline running on overdrive, burning through my energy supply.

And now here I am, at the start of the game.

I take a seat on the bench, and it doesn't take long to figure out this is not going to be a game full of drama. Early in the second half, we are already up 4–0 when Aly Wagner, our attacking midfielder, chips a perfect ball to Tiffeny, who is making a run on the left side. Tiffeny controls and sees that the Ukrainian keeper, Veronika Shulha, is well off her line. Tiffeny pops a left-footed ball over Shulha's head into the unguarded net, an artful goal from an artful player. The crowd goes nuts, and Tiffeny celebrates and cradles the ball. She's only the sixth U.S. woman to reach the one-hundred-goal mark.

A minute or two after Tiffeny scores her historic goal, Greg Ryan looks down the bench.

"Carli, start warming up," he says. I peel off my warm-ups and begin the soccer substitute ritual, stretching and twisting and running, back and forth over the same sliver of sideline. At the next stoppage of play, Greg tells me to go in for Aly. I am standing on the edge of the Merlo Field pitch, trying to breathe and remembering James's words.

Just go out and play . . . Let your training do the talking . . . Keep it simple.

Play finally stops. It is the sixty-fourth minute. I'm about to make my first cap — my first appearance with the national team.

Aly comes off, and I give her a quick hug and run out into the midfield. Play resumes. I get involved quickly. I make a couple of tackles and connect on a few short passes. The nerves gradually recede. Soon I am not first-cap Carli anymore; I am just a soccer player. Minutes go by and I start taking more risks, making a backheel pass and taking on people. As time winds down, I beat a defender and make a quick run up the middle and thread a ball to Heather O'Reilly, fellow New Jerseyan and the youngest player on the team. Heather scored not more than a few minutes earlier, and it looks as if this might be another one, but her shot goes just wide.

The referee blows the whistle three times, signaling the end of the match. As Tiffeny Milbrett gets ready to be honored and interviewed by the press, I grab a ball to commemorate the occasion. Everybody signs it. Somebody writes, "The first of many." I like the sound of that.

Even before my first cap, 2005 is shaping up as a game-changer of a year. A new coach takes over the U-21s, and I get an invite to training camp in preparation for another Nordic Cup (the rules allow each team to bring in a couple of over-age players, and I am one of them). The coach's name is Jill Ellis. She has a great reputation, having built UCLA into a national power that would go to seven straight College Cups.

We steamroll through the Nordic Cup for a record seventh straight victory, beating Germany 3–1 in the third game to win our group and then blowing out Norway, 4–1, in the final. The German coach tells Jill we are one of the best U-21 teams he has ever seen.

I finish my best Nordic Cup with three goals and two assists in the four games. Not long after, I get my first payday as a soccer player—a $5,000 Athlete Support Grant from the U.S. Olympic Committee.

The money does not change my life. I do not immediately go out and buy a new house or a car. Still, it's a huge deal to me, an affirmation that things are heading in the right direction and that I am actually becoming an adult. I celebrate by buying a flat-screen TV for my room at home. I'm not there much to watch it, but it feels good to know I bought it with money I made from playing soccer.

I am still a young woman in a big hurry. I want this to happen now, and it's almost a daily wrestling match to keep reminding myself of Danielle Fotopoulos's words about how hard it is to break through, how you have to keep grinding it out—or, as James tells me over and over, keep emptying the tank every time you play.

It sounds as simple as tic-tac-toe, I know, but the whole process is fraught with so much anxiety that I need the constant reminders.

And nobody knows that better than James.

Before every training camp or major competition, he

writes me a long email, offering positive reinforcement and underscoring the same key themes. I read them over and over, hardwiring them into my brain. It's such a blessing to have a trainer who is so wise and giving.

"All players at the national level have talent; it's the ones with character who end up making it," James writes before I head off to a camp in 2005. "Character that shows that you are willing to do whatever it takes to win. Character that shows that you will play as the coach asks and [you're] a player that gives the coach undivided attention when in the huddle and at team meetings. It is important that you show all these signs although they are not things you do with the ball.

"Make sure you show the coaches that you are there to be a winner and not another talent going to waste."

|||||

I get my second career cap in Charleston, South Carolina, where we play Mexico in a friendly in late October. I come on in the second half, again for Aly Wagner. With a 3–0 lead already on the board (thanks to a goal by Kristine Lilly and two by Abby Wambach), I am ready to heed James's words and show character and do whatever needs to be done to seal the victory. We have not allowed a goal for the entire year and don't want to mess this up in our final game of 2005, so we stay compact and fend off the Mexicans' attempts to get an attack going.

In the closing minutes, I am controlling the ball near the 18-yard line when I see Shannon MacMillan making a run on the right. I slip the ball through to her. Shannon hits a hard shot that the Mexican keeper makes a kick-save on. About a minute later, it's my turn to fire, also from the right side of the penalty area. I hit a hard shot as I am knocked to the ground. The keeper blocks it, and I pop up and one-time the rebound, only to be stopped again.

The referee is about to blow his whistle to end it when I get the ball again, now about thirty yards out. I love to shoot from distance. It can't be anything but good for me to show Greg Ryan the kind of threat I can be in midfield. I take a full-throttle swing at the ball, coming through so hard that I completely lose my balance. The ball skies high enough that it could hit a seagull, and I go down. I land on my left wrist and hear it crack.

The whistle blows.

The game is over, and I am off to see the team doctors and get an X-ray. I don't need pictures to know what happened. My wrist is broken. The pain is throbbing. I am out for six weeks, and I am sick about it. The only good thing is that we have no more camps or games.

One doctor I visit thinks I should have surgery, but the U.S. Soccer medical staff is convinced it will heal fully on its own. All I need to do is put a cast on it. That sounds good to me. I want to get back to training and playing as soon as I can, because 2006 is going to be a big year.

We begin with a January camp and a trip to China, the start of a process that will have a major impact on who Greg Ryan selects to play in the World Cup in 2007. I don't have a great read on what Greg thinks of me as a player. I do know that he has a defensive mentality and that I am going to have to prove to him that I am a full-service, two-way midfielder. The proving needs to start right away. I can't leave any doubt.

6

COACH'S CROSSHAIRS

I AM A WORRIER by nature. I could've majored in over-thinking at Rutgers if it were an option. The matter that I am overanalyzing at the moment is this:

Why does Greg Ryan hate me?

Why is he always on my case, and why can't I ever seem to please him?

It's the beginning of 2006 and my wrist is healed, but my soccer confidence feels as if it's been flattened by an eighteen-wheeler. We have a camp in January, and I make the roster to travel to China for the Four Nations Cup, my first international trip with the full national team. The good news ends there.

I barely play at all, and when I do, I feel as though Greg Ryan is all over my case, mostly about my defense.

That is his highest priority. He is a coach whose preferred style is lockdown defense on one end and bruising, direct offense on the other. I know how important it is to defend; I've known it ever since Chris Petrucelli cut me precisely because I wasn't up to his standards in that area. James has been pounding that into me from day one on Ark Road. Still, an attacking midfielder is supposed to attack, no? Shouldn't she be able to carve the defense up and spread the ball around the field and be a threat in the attacking third?

I guess not, since Greg seems completely unimpressed with what I can offer when I am on the ball.

"You can't give her so much room."

"You can't stab in like that."

"You can't just play in one direction when you are in the midfield."

These are things I hear constantly from Greg Ryan. His ideal midfielder seems to be Shannon Boxx, who is very much a defensive-minded player. All I seem to hear is "Great job, Shannon," and "Way to defend, Shannon." The coach is right; Shannon is a defensive workhorse, and she is incredibly valuable because of that. I am not questioning that at all.

I *am* questioning where that leaves me with Greg Ryan, and so I commence with the overthinking, stressing over my lack of playing time and trying to figure out how I can change Greg's mind. I get back to the States, and James goes to work on me.

"Don't worry about what you can't control, mate," James says. "Just keep emptying the tank and getting better. Everything else will take care of itself."

So I start training again with James, but as I do, I have some business stuff to sort out. I'm under contract with U.S. Soccer now and also have endorsement interest from Nike, Puma, and Adidas. It's another sign that I am no longer just a kid who loves soccer; I am a professional soccer player.

I need an agent to handle this for me, and it just so happens that Rich Fornaro, my mother's cousin, is an attorney. My mother works for Rich in his office in Hamilton, New Jersey. Rich is a sharp guy, a very likable guy. He has been handling some of the initial business offerings informally, but now it is time to firm things up. My parents have no doubt that Rich is the man for the job, and I'm good with it.

"It's great that we can keep this in the family and have someone representing you who we can completely trust," my father tells me. Then he calls James.

"My wife and I have discussed it, and we've decided Rich has got to be the one to represent Carli," my father says. "He's a family guy, and my wife works for him, and it just makes sense all the way around."

James says, "That's fine with me, mate. As long as Carli is on board, we're good."

On a Saturday night in the spring, we all have dinner at Rich's house, a ceremonial closing of our working relationship.

A little time passes, and I am training with James, getting ready for the next camp, an important proving ground for me with World Cup qualifying beginning in the latter part of the year.

I can't say I know exactly what the trigger is, but I gradually begin to have some second thoughts about working with Rich. What if some problem or issue comes up? Could that jeopardize my mom's job? Wouldn't it be awkward for everybody? Couldn't it also wind up hurting me that he is not a sports agent and doesn't know the legal landscape in that area? I've had these endorsement opportunities for some time, and still no agreement has been reached.

I'm also starting to question my parents' involvement in every aspect of my soccer.

I will always love my parents for all their sacrifices of time and money to help me. I am very grateful to them. But now I am twenty-four years old, and more and more, their input seems to put a strain on our relationship.

When I come back from a camp, I am often grilled with questions. *How did you play? How was your body language? Did you connect with the other players?* These camps are exhausting and mentally grinding all by themselves. Having to give a full debriefing isn't something I have much patience for.

"I really don't want to talk about it," I say. "I just have to keep working hard."

This answer always sets my parents off.

The issue that my parents harp on above all others is making sure I play the political game, being nice and forging alliances with influential veteran players. I want to make the team because of my skills and not because of who my friends are.

"I don't want to be a suck-up," I say.

"That's not what I'm suggesting. I just want you to be smart and give yourself your best chance to succeed," my father says.

I have never been somebody to go with the crowd. My parents appreciated that quality in high school, when lots of other kids were going to parties while I was getting sleep so I could be ready for my next training session. It's not about being antisocial or rude. It's about putting in the effort on the field and getting where I want to go. If that means missing out on parties or social events, hey, I'm going to do whatever it takes.

My mother would caution me at times about being too much of a loner and not going out with my teammates.

"Mom, going out to a party is not what's going to get

me on the national team. Staying back and resting and being ready to kick butt the next day and showing the coach I'm emptying the tank—that's what is going to get me on the national team."

Briana Scurry, the great goalkeeper who helped the U.S. capture the 1999 World Cup, is my roommate on one of our road trips. I ask her if she talks to her family about her soccer career, and if they are involved at all in the business side of it.

"I never talk to them about any of it," she says. "I love my family, but they don't understand. I never want to mix family and business."

Bri has been around a lot longer than I have. Her point makes complete sense to me. I call James.

"I've been thinking it over, and I am not sure I want to go with Rich after all," I tell him. "I'm just not comfortable with it." I tell him about my conversation with Bri. I bring up my concern about what would happen to my mother's job if things don't go well. Most of all, I think it's important to have someone with experience in the soccer world and who knows the finer points of endorsement deals.

Nothing against Rich, but this is not his area of expertise. James knows Rich well and likes him as much as I do. James agrees that my points are valid.

"What are you going to do?" James asks.

"I'm going to tell Rich that I've been reconsidering things and I think I am going to explore other options," I tell him.

I reach out to Rich and explain my thinking. I tell him that I feel badly about changing my mind, but my gut tells me this is the right decision.

Rich is totally classy about it.

"I understand completely," Rich says. "You have to go with what makes the most sense and makes you most comfortable."

I am hugely relieved, but my parents are incensed. It's the first completely independent decision I've made in my life, and my parents think I've blown it bigtime.

"I just don't want you to lose your job in case something breaks down," I try to explain to my mother. "At the end of the day, I just think it's risky to mix family and business. I am just not comfortable with the entire thing."

Nothing I am saying is registering. None of us is very good at handling anger and other strong emotions. Like a lot of families, we wind up getting our backs up and our egos involved. Then listening stops and accusations start flying. I am as guilty as anybody.

I storm out of the house.

The situation isn't good. James is concerned that if things fester, it would not only be terrible for the family; it could also mess up my head and affect my performance. He wants me to sit down with my parents and try to explain things again and see if we can smooth over some of the anger and hurt.

"That's fine, but I want you to be there, because I don't think I'll be able to get my points across if you are not," I say.

James agrees, and we arrange for the four of us to get together for dinner at a place called Prospectors, a western-themed steakhouse and dance hall on Ark Road, just down the road from James's training fields. The last thing we want to do is meet in Delran, where we'd probably know half the people in the place.

It is a Monday night, at six thirty. The place is empty, but we get an out-of-the-way table anyway, just to ensure our privacy. I am trying to be positive, but the truth is I am dreading this.

My parents and James are sitting at the table when I arrive.

James says, "I don't enjoy being in the middle of a family issue, but Carli invited me to come because she was afraid this thing would blow up. I'm just here to help, and I know you guys are upset about what's happened with Rich."

My father says to me, "I think what you did to Rich is wrong, but honestly that's not what we really care about. Our biggest concern is the way you disrespect your mother and me. It's almost like you're not the same daughter we raised and supported all these years."

He gives a quick rundown of all the times I've mouthed off, not answered calls or emails, kept them at a distance.

I try to offer my side of things, but my father keeps going, talking right over me.

My frustration is building by the second. Suddenly, I snap. I push back my chair and stand up.

"I came here to try to work things out, not to find out how terrible a person I am," I say. Then I storm out.

It's not the most mature move of my life, but I don't know what else to do. As I said, I don't always do well with anger.

In that moment, I just feel helpless, as if I'll never be heard or have my feelings respected. I feel bulldozed.

I am so sad that it has come to this.

I call Brian, and he comes and picks me up.

The fight in the corner of Prospectors stays with me a long time. We've had our spats before, sure, but this is a deeper cut. It's far beyond feeling rejected or misunderstood.

I stick to my plan to look for a different agent. Not long after, I hire John Johnson of Cozen O'Connor. It turns out to be one of the best moves I've ever made.

|||||

The next big tournament is the Algarve Cup in March in Portugal. In the second of the four games, Greg Ryan gives me my first start in a 5—0 rout of Denmark. I help set up one of Heather O'Reilly's two goals and feel pretty good about my performance. Greg is still on me a lot about my defense, but every day I show up and work. I believe I am gradually winning him over.

I start again in the final against Germany. I bang a shot off the left post from distance in the first half. The game remains scoreless and goes to PKs, the Germans finally prevailing, 4—3. It stinks to lose, but it's impossible not to see that I am making progress. I just started two of four games — including the final — of one of the most important competitions of the year.

A couple of days later, I get an email from Greg.

"You had a fantastic tournament," he writes. "You should gain a lot of confidence from your performance in Portugal. Do not be satisfied as your potential is way ahead of you. Keep learning every time you step into a training session or a game. You have a great future with this team if you keep giving everything in you."

Greg's email is the most affirming assessment I've ever gotten from him. If only things were as positive at home. On the surface, my parents and I are getting along a little better. That is encouraging, but the deep, underlying divide remains. My parents are angry and resentful that I am closing them out of my soccer career; I am angry and resentful that they refuse to let me take full ownership of my soccer career.

I understand that our whole family life revolved around my travels and tournaments for years, and that my brother and sister got short shrift as a result.

It doesn't mean that my parents get to tell me what to do for the rest of my life.

I keep trying to make this point, and it never seems to get through. This is my journey. If I fall, I have to be the one to pick myself up. If I'm not getting the playing time I want or not impressing the coach, it's up to me to figure out why. Every time something goes wrong doesn't mean it's time for a family discussion; it means I have to get better, make better decisions, and get back to the place that will take me where I want to go. If Greg is all over the place in his opinion of me as a player, I just have to work harder and eliminate any doubts he might have.

The problem with my parents is compounded by my father's frequent critiques of my game. My dad was my first coach, the coach who launched me on my way. Of course he wants me to do well, but sometimes it is too much for me to take in.

A week after my twenty-fourth birthday, we play a friendly against Ireland in San Diego. I fly my parents out and put them up in a hotel so they can watch the game. Shannon Boxx, our stalwart holding mid, is out with an injury, and Kristine Lilly is out too. So I know I am going to have to shoulder much more of the defensive responsibilities.

We come out flying, peppering the Irish goal with shots. In the twentieth minute, I slip a pass down the left wing to forward Christie Welsh, who crosses to a charging Heather O'Reilly. Heather knocks it in. Defender Cat Whitehill pounds in a rebound, and we're up 2–0 at the half, on our way to a 5–0 victory.

I meet my parents briefly after the game.

"You didn't play like yourself," my father says. "You've gone away from the creative, attacking game you've always played."

"Dad, I'm playing the way the coach wants me to play," I say. "He wants me to be a ball-winner and be as active on defense as I am on offense."

The standoff continues.

IIIII

I want to believe that I will resolve things with my parents eventually, but right now my focus is on firming up my spot on the roster. I need to get ready for World Cup qualifying.

I have solid games starting in late-summer victories over

China and Mexico and then earn my fifteenth cap in a friendly in the Home Depot Center in Carson, California, against Chinese Taipei. The game is October 1, 2006, almost a year to the day since the start of the World Cup in China, and it is not what you'd call a stiff challenge. We get off twenty-three shots to none for Chinese Taipei. Abby Wambach records her fifth hat trick and adds three assists. In the seventy-sixth minute, with the score 7–0, Abby gets a ball with her back to the goal, about thirty yards out, and one-times the ball out to the right, where I am making a run. It is a perfect pass. I run onto it in full stride, fire, and slot it into the lower far corner. I make a little half-hop in delight — anything more would've been tacky, given the score — and my teammates rush up to congratulate me.

It is my first goal for the U.S. Women's National Team, the biggest moment I've had since I made my debut in Portland fifteen months earlier. Not unlike that first cap, it is surreal to be in my boots as I run back upfield, trying to get my head around the fact that I just scored a goal for the United States of America.

Three minutes later, Megan Rapinoe, a rising twenty-one-year-old star who is still a senior in college, follows with the first goal of her career (and adds number two a few minutes after that). It is our eighth straight victory after the PK loss to Germany in the Algarve Cup final, improving our 2006 record to 13-1-1.

Everything should be looking great, except that I am back in Greg Ryan's doghouse. We head off to South Korea for three games. We play Denmark first. The coaches tell me right before the game is starting that they want me to man-mark a Danish player. Almost from the first whistle to the last, Greg is yelling at me.

"You're giving her too much space, Carli."

"Tighten up on her."

"Carli, we need you to defend."

At halftime, Greg reams me out some more, and then says, "I'm going to give you another chance to go out there and get it right."

I work hard and think I stay on the Danish woman pretty effectively, but Greg definitely does not agree. The game ends in a 1–1 draw, and we look awful. I don't play in the next game against Australia. When we have a midfielders' meeting, Greg lets me have it one more time.

"Your defense is really hurting us. You are making us vulnerable over and over again, and it's got to stop," he says.

I don't mind being criticized and will listen to anything that I think will help make me a better player, but I honestly feel Greg is way off on this. I probably should keep my mouth shut.

But I don't.

"I think my defending is getting better. I don't think defending is our problem."

Greg glares at me, his face reddening. Now he is screaming at me.

"Your defending is horrible! You don't know what you are talking about! We looked terrible against Denmark, and if you don't see that, you are clueless."

I am as angry as he is now. The meeting breaks up, and he tells me to hang around. It's just the two of us.

"Don't you ever question me like that again in front of other players," he says. "You have no right to do that. You make me look bad, and you make yourself look like a bad teammate, someone who thinks she is bigger than the team. You better knock it off or you are going to have a very short career with the national team."

I almost start crying on the spot but hold it together until I get back to my room. I completely lose it and start bawling my head off. Even more than Greg's harsh words, what upsets me is that I have no idea where I stand with him. He changes moods and evaluations the way most people change socks.

I believe — I know — I am a better defensive player, a harder-working player, than I was back in the spring when he wrote me that glowing email. But am I wrong about that? Am I going backwards, or is he trying to motivate me?

I was totally, utterly wrong to mouth off; that only made things worse. I let my frustration get the better of me.

I have to do better.

IIIII

I am back in the starting lineup for the last two games of the South Korea trip. We win them both, against the Netherlands and Canada. Greg isn't on me as much, but I can't be sure it's because I'm playing better.

We head back to the States and our home base, the Home Depot Center, for the biggest tournament I've played to date in my short time with the national team — the CONCACAF Gold Cup, which serves as the World Cup qualifier.

Our opener is against Mexico in late November. I go the full ninety minutes in a 2–0 victory, and overall it is one of my best efforts yet. I defend well, tackle hard, and spray balls all over the park — one-touch passes here and through balls there. I ping balls across the field and put pressure on the Mexican defense. Best of all, the victory assures us of a spot in the World Cup the following year in China. We finish the tournament by defeating Canada in overtime, 2–1, and it's a little extra sweet because James comes out to watch in person. It is great to have him there and meet everybody.

When James congratulates Greg on the Gold Cup victory, Greg has a moment with him.

"Please make sure Carli gets some time off and rests up. Next year is going to be a long grind," Greg says.

The team takes a holiday break, and I head back to South Jersey. I don't tell Greg, and I'm sure James doesn't either, but there's no way I'm backing off. A couple of days to recharge is all I need, and then James and I head for the Blue Barn, our winter training location in Marlton, New Jersey. It's a tin-sided place that sits off Tuckerton Road and looks as if it could double as an airplane hangar. I keep going back to the truth I learned when I started working with James: I am not naturally fit, so I need to do more physical training than just about anybody. I need to keep adding cords of muscles, build endurance, and sharpen and tighten all my ball skills.

Rest?

I don't think so.

7

WORLD OF TROUBLE

I HAVE TWO NEW BEST friends as 2007 begins. One is my roommate for yet another trip to China, Marci Miller. Marci is seven years older than me, a person I immediately trust and connect with. Both of us are homebodies who don't care about hanging out until all hours. Instead, Marci and I stay in our room and watch movies.

We encourage each other constantly, even though we are both center midfielders and theoretically competing for playing time.

Being with Marci is like being back with the Medford Strikers girls. She always has my back, the same way the Strikers did. The national team has a much different team dynamic, often a much less pleasant one. People seem to be threatened by me and aren't eager to see me do well because I might take their spot. I experience a culture of wariness instead of warmth.

Early in my time with the team, I made a run in the attacking third and was wide open but did not get the ball. I didn't think anything of it at the time, until it happened again and again.

Finally, it dawned on me that I didn't get the ball because this teammate did not want me to have it, never mind that I might do something good with it. No, the pass instead went another way, from one friend to another. The realization was stunning to me, and sad.

Do players on the U.S. Women's National Team really make decisions on who they pass to based on who they like, or based on whose position they are trying to protect? I wondered.

I asked someone I had gotten to know and trust if I was being paranoid.

"No, you are not being paranoid at all," she said.

You want to think that the higher up you go in a sport, political stuff will become less important and everything will be about how good you are. You want to believe the best players make the U.S. Women's National Team, and the best of those will be the starters.

I'm not saying that any of the women on the U.S. national team didn't earn their spots; every person who makes the team is a gifted player. All I'm saying is that we are not always viewed through the same lens. If some players lose the ball or don't execute a pass well, it is typically overlooked. If I commit the same mistake, it is a big fat strike against me and usually will get me pulled out of the game. The burden is on me if I want to change the pecking order.

For a long time, I resent that. I feel slighted and unappreciated.

With James's help, I start to use it as motivation.

You don't think I am good enough? You don't think I'm the player who should be your starter at attacking mid?

I will show you.

It is not the first time that an industrial-sized chip on my shoulder works to my advantage.

Whatever politics and preconceptions may exist within the team, I don't want to have any part of such nonsense. I have no hidden agendas. I want to play my best, and I want to win. It's that simple.

Marci is the same way. There isn't any drama about her. She is a soccer player, a darn good one.

I wish Marci could be my teammate forever, but I know that won't be the case. Indeed, not long after the World Cup, she departs the national team to take a coaching position at Northern Illinois University.

My other new friend is Michele Gould, our physical therapist on the trip to China. On the second practice of the trip, I block a blast of a shot by teammate Lori Chalupny. The force of it jerks my foot outward and results in the worst sprained ankle I've ever had. Michele has me in ice buckets four or five times a day. When my foot isn't in the bucket, Michele puts it in a compression wrap or is massaging it to stimulate blood flow so it will heal faster. Michele is a savior. If she weren't with us, I don't think I would have even gotten on the field.

It's not a serious injury by any means, but the experience is a reminder of the importance of taking care of your body. The strength and vitality of your body are where it all starts. You need to listen to it and let it heal when it needs to heal.

It's also a reminder of how invisible you become when you are not playing. Watching practice, I feel as useful as a deflated ball. The week that I am out, Greg pays no attention to me, and why would he? I am not playing. I am not out there training and helping the team get better.

When I am finally back to work, I come off the field after a training session.

"How's your ankle?" Greg asks.

"It feels good. I'm ready to go," I say.

"Well, you don't look good," he says.

His comment really ticks me off, and I walk away. I've worked my tail off to get back, and all he can tell me is I don't look good? I know I am doing myself no favors with this reaction. I am still immature, headstrong. My default response to a coach who is riding me this hard is to pull away and shut him out. Being coachable is one of things I am still trying to learn.

I come off the bench in the first game, a scoreless tie against Germany, and I don't play well. I lose the ball a few times and try to force things too much. In our second game, against England, Marci gets banged up, and I come on for her. I play much better, but then Greg and I have words after he yells something on the field and thinks I am disregarding him. Afterward, Greg and I have a clear-the-air session. Bret Hall, Greg's top assistant, is there in case we need a mediator.

Greg tells me I am not coachable at times, and he needs to know I will hear him out and abide by his wishes.

I tell him that I feel that I can't do anything right, and I am trying so hard to please him that it's taking away the fun of playing.

The conversation doesn't brush away the problems, but at least we've had a civil and honest dialogue and know how we both feel. After we return to the States, we have a residency camp in February, and Greg has individual meetings with us and asks us about our goals. I tell him I want to master free kicks, be more of an offensive force, and do everything I can to continue to improve as a player.

"My long-term goal is to be World Player of the Year," I say.

Greg chuckles. I can tell he's trying to stifle an all-out laugh, hearing this coming from the mouth of a twenty-four-year-old who isn't even established in the starting lineup yet. I know it must sound incredibly audacious and arrogant, but I don't care. That is the truth. That is what James and I have talked about from the beginning.

It is what I've been visualizing almost from the first day on Ark Road.

"You must be able to see it happening in your mind before it can happen on the field," James said to me then, and many times since.

The mind is like a brush-cutter in the woods, he says. It clears away the brambles and thickets so you have a path to follow. The mind sets out the path, and the training enables you to follow it.

This is our plan, and I am sticking with it.

|||||

Next, the team heads to Portugal for the Algarve Cup, where we open up against China. It's a 1–1 game late in the first half when Abby Wambach crosses the ball from the right, through the penalty area toward the left corner. Stephanie Lopez runs the ball down and nutmegs her defender before toe-poking a pass back to me. I juke a defender and crack a right-footed shot from twenty-five yards out into the upper left corner.

It turns out to be the game-winner and sets me on my way. We win all four games, and I score in every one of them. I am named tournament MVP and Top Goal Scorer. It is easily the high point of my young career. My confidence soars as we ramp up our preparation for the World Cup.

Maybe this will be a turning point in my career and in my relationship with Greg, I think.

Usually the more time you spend around a person, the better you get to know them. With Greg, the more time I spend around him, the more confused I become. I never know if he's going tell me that I am on my way to being a world-class midfielder or that I am an embarrassment who is lucky to have a spot on his roster.

None of us has any luck reading him. When we come out for practice, our running joke is, "Who is he going to crush today?" The funny thing is when Greg was April Heinrich's assistant, we all loved him. He was our pal. He moved over to coach, and everything changed.

After a closed-door scrimmage against Japan in San Jose, California, in late July, Greg is profoundly unhappy and wants us to know it. We are all sitting on the ground in front of him. He is standing over us with his barrel chest and massive calves. Greg played professionally for the North American Soccer League and Major Indoor Soccer League; they are not top pro leagues, but Greg was a rugged defender. You have to respect that. Greg Ryan is nobody to mess with.

"All of you who were part of the 2004 Olympic team, sit over here," he says, pointing to a line on the field. "You guys—Chupa [Lori Chalupny], Leslie [Osborne], and Marci—you go over there," he continues, pointing in a different direction.

You can feel an explosion coming.

"These are people who will fight for each other and for me and do whatever it takes to win," he says, referring to the two groups. Then he looks at the rest of us—Hope Solo, Tina Ellertson, Nicole Barnhart, Natasha Kai, and me—and screams, "You are people who don't have heart and don't work hard and don't care about the team."

I am so stunned I don't know what to say. I have been criticized before, but this is at a different level. No heart? Don't care about the team? I don't want to talk about this with the other players who are singled out. I don't want to talk to anybody. When Greg is finally done, I grab my stuff and head straight for the bus. I am far from a perfect player. I know I have so much to learn. But for him to tell us that we have no heart and don't work hard and don't put the team first, well, that is not true and not fair. Yes, he's the coach and I'm the player, but it is still completely ridiculous. If it is meant to motivate us, it's even worse.

It doesn't motivate me. It depresses me.

Greg Ryan is under a great deal of pressure; I understand that. His team is a heavy favorite to bring home the first World Cup since 1999. If we don't deliver, it's on him. I know he wants to keep us humble and hungry. I just don't think constantly demeaning people is the way to achieve that.

Greg stays on my case for the rest of the summer. His criticisms focus on my defense and my tendency to take risks and take people on. My head is spinning. James sends a series of texts and emails to keep me grounded, and Marci reinforces them. When she sees how upset I am one day, she texts me and says, "You need to keep believing in what you can do. Everyone thinks you are so damn good. . . . Something great is coming your way."

The words help, and my new, self-designed Nike cleats give me a little emotional pickup too. I'm the first female Nike athlete to design her own cleats for the World Cup.

I have three different designs. I have a red-white-and-blue pair for the first round and a yellow pair for the quarters and semis, with the Five Pillars of Universal Soccer Academy in the back. For the finals, I have an orange pair. They stand for all my supporters and loved ones. James's initials, JG, are on the tongue, and 143 is on the side for Brian, our private code for *I love you*.

I don't know whether my shoes and I are going to start, but I feel fit and strong and ready to go. My parents and Brian have made the trip, and even with the problems my parents and I have been having, I appreciate that they will be in China to support me. Brian is so loyal and kind; it's comforting to know he will be there for me as well.

I am rooming with Marci again, so I'm happy about that. One of the first things I do when we settle into our room is watch a film clip given to me by Phil Wheddon, our goalkeeping coach. It's a personal highlight reel — Phil gives one to each player — and it helps with my mental imaging. I see myself ripping shots from distance, delivering crunching tackles, and threading through balls. Phil does a masterful job with the clip. I watch it often.

Greg has been the coach for eighteen months now, in which time we have not lost a single game in regulation time. We've won forty-five games and lost one. Yet to me we still don't seem settled and confident as a team, even with the leadership of Kristine Lilly, the goal-scoring prowess of Abby

Wambach, and the emergence of Hope Solo as an elite goal-keeper.

Ten days before the World Cup is to kick off against Korea in Chengdu, Greg gathers us together and announces that we're changing formation from a 4-2-4 to a 4-3-3, adding an extra player in midfield. He sounds excited about it and tells me it means I am back in the starting lineup. I am wondering if he is messing with me or if he really means it.

It turns out he means it.

The opener against Korea, the youngest team in the field, doesn't go the way we hope. It's a rainy, sloppy field, and the Koreans get the better of us through most of the first half. I win a ball in midfield and feed it to Lilly, who steers a pass on the right to Abby. She opens the scoring in the fiftieth minute. But then Abby knocks heads defending our goal a few minutes later and suffers a nasty gash that requires eleven stitches. Greg doesn't want to lose Abby, so he opts not to sub, and Korea strikes twice when she's out, the first on a shot beyond the 18 that slips through Hope's hands. Heather O'Reilly ties the score with a surgical one-touch strike off a loose ball into the upper right corner in the sixty-ninth minute, sparing us an unthinkable defeat.

I'm not happy with the tie, but I am happy with my performance. I defend and win fifty-fifty balls and help orchestrate things offensively.

"You grew a lot as a player in this game. That was an excellent first World Cup game," Greg says.

We win our second game 2–0 over Sweden on two more goals by Abby, but the truth is that we still don't look our best. We're playing ugly, direct football—Greg's preferred style—bypassing the midfield and launching long balls to Abby or Lilly and hoping for the best. Our defense is tight, and Hope throws a shutout, and though I get subbed out for Shannon Boxx, I believe I've turned in another creditable effort.

We leave Chengdu for Shanghai, where we grind out a 1–0 victory over Nigeria to advance out of our group. I start a third straight game, this time getting subbed for Leslie Osborne. Greg seems to sense my frustration with the way we are not connecting passes or playing possession soccer.

Greg approaches me later and asks if we can talk.

"I just want to check in and see how you are doing," he says. "I know I've been tough on you the last two and a half years, and I am so proud of how you've come along. You are going to be the future of this team."

It is one second later, maybe two, that he informs me that

I will not be starting in our first elimination game against England.

It's official: I will never understand this man.

As we get ready for the game, Greg wants to build morale and quiet any rumblings of discontent about how we are playing.

"We're outplaying every team in this tournament and haven't given up a goal in 11 v. 11 play. Not one," he says, reminding us that Korea's two goals came with Abby off the field for ten minutes.

Then we players have our own meeting, and it becomes very clear how deep the frustration goes. Abby says we are focusing too much on defense and need to be more aggressive offensively, no matter what Greg says.

"I feel like I can't play-make or build up the attack because we're just sending long balls to the forward line," I say.

Just about everybody speaks up, and the unrest is as thick as the China smog.

But you wouldn't know it watching the England game, which we blow open with three goals in twelve minutes early in the second half. I only play ten minutes and can't say that I understand why, but the mayhem is just beginning.

We've advanced to the semifinals against Brazil, a rising power in the sport with a collection of dazzlingly skilled players. They play like jazz musicians in cleats, riffing and improvising as they go. Brazil is led by Marta, a twenty-year-old superstar, and teammates Cristiane and Formiga (when you are a big soccer star in Brazil, no second name is necessary). The Brazilians have scored thirteen goals in four games. Still, we are the top-ranked team in the world, and even though there are many new faces on this team, we are considered a strong favorite to win it all.

It is the most anticipated match of the 2007 World Cup, and it becomes even more so when Greg Ryan does one more shocking about-face, replacing Hope with Briana Scurry in goal. After a shaky start against Korea, Hope had recorded three straight shutouts. She has been our starter for a couple of years. Bri is a legendary keeper, a former World Cup champion, and an Olympic champion, but it is unprecedented to make such a switch at this point in a World Cup. Greg's explanation is that Bri is a superior shot-stopper and has a brilliant track record against Brazil.

Hope is fuming, crushed. She gets even more upset when she learns that apparently Lilly and Abby had lobbied for the goalkeeping change.

I don't get it, because I think Hope is the best keeper in the world. I still don't get how the drama keeps seeping to the surface like so much toxic waste with this team.

The biggest match of the tournament begins with an own-goal in the twentieth minute, when Leslie Osborne tries to clear a corner kick with a low header and winds up putting it past Bri into our goal. Bri hasn't played a game in three months and looks rusty, tentative. How could she not? Then Marta wins a ball in our end and attacks, cutting into the box and firing a low, left-footed shot toward the right post. Bri gets a hand on it, but her reaction isn't quite quick enough. It's 2–0, Brazil, and when Shannon Boxx gets sent off for a second yellow card—a complete phantom call on a play when she is the one who was fouled—we are looking at playing the second forty-five minutes down a man.

I come on in the second half for Stephanie Lopez, but we are mostly playing desperate, skill-less soccer. In the seventy-ninth minute, Marta schools us again, flicking a pass to herself, wheeling around Tina Ellertson, carving up Cat Whitehill with a cutback, and beating Bri on the near side. We wind up losing, 4–0. It is not just our first defeat in more than eighteen months. It's the worst Women's World Cup loss in U.S. history. I'm still trying to figure out how things unraveled so fast when I hear that Hope has just ripped Greg and Bri in a postmatch interview.

"It was the wrong decision," Hope says. "And I think

anybody that knows anything about the game knows that. There's no doubt in my mind I would have made those saves. And the fact of the matter is, it's not 2004 anymore. It's not 2004. It's 2007, and I think you have to live in the present. And you can't live by big names. You can't live in the past. It doesn't matter what somebody did in an Olympic gold medal game three years ago. Now is what matters, and that's what I think."

Aaron Heifetz, our press officer, had tried to stop Hope from talking to the press, but Hope ignored him. In less time than it takes Marta to make one of her spin moves, outrage sweeps through our team and Hope is an instant pariah. She's isolated at our team meal and barred from our third-place game against Norway. She isn't welcome in the medal ceremony to get the bronzes we didn't want. She isn't even allowed to fly home with the team.

"You wouldn't believe what's going on. Everybody is freaking out," I tell James in a text.

James tells me the Hope saga is all over the media at home, too.

Hope is summoned to a meeting with the veterans, and they let her have it for breaking ranks and criticizing a revered teammate. Hope apologizes, but it is not enough. They want her to pay for her breach, and then pay some more.

Hope is my closest friend on the team. She was directing her tirade at Greg, and it almost came out as a rant against Bri. Still, I think this full-blown freeze-out is taking things too far.

In men's sports, people criticize coaches and managers all the time and sometimes call out teammates, too, and it's not that huge a deal. Things get hot, and then it goes away. Often the guy speaking out is even lauded for having the courage to tell the truth.

When it happens in women's sports, though, it always seems to be viewed as a nasty, claws-out catfight. I hate that our World Cup has devolved into this, but I am not going to be part of the Hate Hope Campaign. I am not going to abandon my friend. It's a gang mentality, and the gang wants to do everything but put Hope in jail.

It's too much. Hope was wrong, but this is even more wrong.

James and I talk it through, and he agrees.

"Hope didn't kill anybody. She expressed an opinion," James said.

And what everybody forgets in their haste to bury Hope is that Briana Scurry once did pretty much the same thing — pointedly criticizing the person she had lost her job to, a goalkeeper named Siri Mullinix. Granted, Bri's comments came a couple of years later, not with the embers of defeat still hot and smoldering, but is there a statute of limitations on team loyalty?

Mullinix was the U.S. starter in the 2000 Olympics in Sydney, where the U.S. lost the gold medal game to Norway, 3–2, due in large part to some shaky goalkeeping. Bri, of course, had been the U.S. keeper for the 1999 World Cup champions, but in the long, happy aftermath had gotten out of shape and lost her job to Mullinix. Sometime before the next World Cup, Bri was asked whether she blamed herself for costing the U.S. the Olympic gold.

"I honestly believe that in my heart, yes. I knew I could've made a difference in that match," she said.

So I refuse to go along. I sit next to Hope. I talk to Hope. I've thought it through, and I completely disagree with this calculated crusade to crush her. I am not backing off that position.

This does not please the anti-Hope cabal at all.

"Be careful about who you align yourself with," somebody says. "It may come back to hurt you."

"I don't care. I am going to stand up for what I think is right," I tell them.

|||||

I do not play one minute against Norway in the third-place game. I sit on the end of the bench for virtually all of the three-game tour we do after the World Cup, watching Aly Wagner play attacking midfield. Do you think this is just a crazy coincidence? I don't.

It is the start of a long period of time in which I am viewed warily by some teammates and almost shunned by others. I am not happy about it. It's not as if I am going out of my way to be an outsider.

But I'm not going to grovel to become part of the in-crowd, either. I am an open book. I have my goals and my routine and a ton of extra work to do to get where I want to go. That is what drives me. Nothing is going to get in the way of that.

I feel very misunderstood by my teammates and wish it weren't so. I don't want them to think I don't like them because I'm not going out with them all the time. There are probably ways I can do more to join in things without jeopardizing my goals. It's something I know I need to work on.

IIIII

We're in the high altitude of Albuquerque, days before our last game of the season, and I need to clear the air with Abby, one of the staunch members of the anti-Hope brigade. I reach out to her and ask if we can talk.

We're in our hotel. She comes to my room. She sits down on the edge of the bed.

"Abby, I respect you as a player and a person," I say. "You've already had a huge impact on this team, and I know that will continue. I don't know what you are hearing about me after all the stuff with Hope, but I just want you to know that I don't want to get dragged into any drama. I just want to help this team win. I work my butt off, whether I am starting or not starting. I leave it all out there every time I am on the field. People may get the wrong idea about me sometimes, because I don't go out and I stay to myself, but being on this team is my dream, and all I want is to contribute however I can to the success the team has had for a long time."

Abby listens quietly. She is a big presence, even when she is sitting in a hotel room. She seems to take in what I am saying, and I think she appreciates the spirit behind it.

Then Abby tells me that she has some things to say too.

"You may not like it, but I hope you will hear me out," she says.

I nod, but I can feel my guard spike.

"This has nothing to do with the Hope situation," Abby

begins. "You expressed your opinion, and that is fine. You are a really good player, but your spot on the team is in jeopardy. You are walking a fine line. You are actually kind of like Hope, because you have to win back the hearts of the team. People don't see you fitting in, chemistry-wise. They see you not wanting to join in things, and just sitting in the corner texting all the time. They feel that you don't trust them, and they don't want you on the field because of that. You also didn't have a very good World Cup, so that adds more questions. You are turning into Hope, and you better be careful."

I am stunned by what I am hearing. Beyond stunned. I know I'm not one of the girls; that much I am clear on. But the other stuff . . . My job is in jeopardy? People don't trust me? They are thinking they don't want me on the team?

I tell Abby that it is hard to have trust right now, with all the stuff going around.

"I do everything I can to work hard, be the best, and not get caught up in the drama. What is so bad about that?"

As far as my World Cup, well, I don't agree. I did as much as I could, considering Greg wanted no part of pretty soccer, possession soccer, and said so himself. I don't want to get into Greg's mood swings either, how hard it is to deal with being the future of the team one day and nothing the next.

I don't get into all this with Abby, because I'm not there to deconstruct Greg's strategy or motivational techniques. I ask Abby if there is anything else.

"Whether we have the same coach or a new coach, you need to know your position is on shaky ground. I hope you can use the time off to look at your mistakes and reevaluate things and come back determined to make things work."

Abby is finally done talking. My insides are seized up. Abby talks a lot, and she lives the way she plays . . . all out, and in your face. She has been a supporter of mine. After I was MVP in the Algarve Cup, she was quoted as saying the tournament was going to change the direction of my career.

I don't think Abby is being mean-spirited by telling me all this, but I do think that she loves to inject herself into the middle of things. I don't appreciate her acting as if she is part of the judge and jury that will decide my future. Yes, I respect Abby and what she brings on the field, but this is way out of bounds.

Abby departs. I stare out the window, trying to get my head around what just happened. My insides churn. I am freaking out, and that is probably understating it. I am terrified that my lifelong dream is in danger of being torpedoed by backroom bickering and backstabbing.

Do these players really have the power to run me off the team?

James and I have a long talk about it. I begin to get some clarity. I need to find out if any of this stuff is true—if I am indeed in a precarious position.

It's not going to change how I work or go about my training, but I still want to know.

I call Cheryl Bailey, the general manager of the U.S. Women's National Team, and ask to meet with Dan Flynn, the CEO of U.S. Soccer.

"You need to speak to Greg before you talk to anyone else," Cheryl says. "He's your immediate boss. That's how we have to start."

I agree and call Greg in the hotel.

"Hey, Greg, this is Carli. I need to talk to you right away. It's important. Do you have a few minutes?"

"Sure, Carli," he says.

Greg and I have had so many ups and downs, and he's under so much pressure in the wake of the Brazil debacle, that I really don't know how he's going to react. I just go straight at it.

"Abby and I just met in my room, and she told me that my spot on the team is in jeopardy and that people don't trust me and don't want to play with me," I say. "Is this true?"

Greg's square face almost seems to freeze before my eyes. He looks genuinely shocked.

"Abby has no right or place telling you your spot is in jeopardy," Greg says. "I don't know where she is coming from, but all I can tell you is that if I am the coach of the team, you are going to be on it. If someone else is the coach of the team, you are going to be on it."

He tells me that if I ever need anything or want to meet with him again to please let him know.

"Thank you, Greg. I really appreciate that," I say. It says a lot about Greg's character that he would go out of his way to reassure me on all this, given our tumultuous history.

The next day, we play poorly and tie Mexico 1–1 to end our year. U.S. Soccer announces after the game that Greg Ryan will not be returning. It is not a decision that surprises anyone. I believe a change has to be made, but I still feel for Greg. I will always be thankful that he was there for me when I needed it.

We say our goodbyes and head our separate ways. We finish 2007 with one loss in twenty-four games, but that loss is viewed as a complete disaster and costs the coach his job. That should give you an idea of the expectations we face. But I don't want to think about the World Cup or the Brazil game or anything else. I just want to get home and see Brian and get back to Ark Road and the Blue Barn and train with James again. Everything else may be in chaos, but that is the one constant. I train with James Galanis; I get better, stronger, fitter. It has been happening for almost four years, and it's not going to change. It is foolproof. Having something in my life that feels foolproof is very comforting right about now.

8

OLYMPIAN AND OUTCAST

THE BEST PART about the end of 2007 is that it leads to
2008. There won't be another World Cup until 2011, of
course, but at least we have the next best thing to look forward to—an opportunity to win our third Olympic gold
medal in the last twelve years. We will go after it under the
direction of a new coach, Pia Sundhage. A former star of the
Swedish national team, she sings Bob Dylan's "The Times
They Are a-Changin'" at our first meeting and talks about a
whole new style of play.

She wants us to dictate tempo, be brave and take risks,
and possess the ball. Talk about music to my ears.

"Let's raise the level of attack in women's soccer," Pia
says.

I love playing for Pia. I am finding new gears in training
because her practices are so fun and challenging. Pia not only
doesn't want to bypass the midfield, she wants everything to

flow through it. She has made it clear she wants me to become a focal point. I am learning so much from her, especially about making runs off the ball and becoming more of a threat that way.

"You have all the tools to become the best player in the world," Pia tells me.

Back for another Algarve Cup a year after I was named MVP, I experience the biggest change of all in the third of our four games, against Norway. I open the tournament with a strong game in a 4–0 victory over China, getting a goal and an assist. I play okay against Italy in our second game, but I am not good against Norway. They pack the middle and sit back on us, putting pressure on our every possession. I never find my rhythm. I am fighting a slight groin pull and don't feel confident. I give away the ball as if I'm handing out Easter eggs, particularly in the first half. But the amazing thing is that Pia doesn't get on me and doesn't pull me.

"I want you to learn to play through games like these," she says.

The second half is better, and we wind up winning, 4–0, and go on to beat Denmark to take the tournament. I feel so fortunate finally to have a coach who seems to appreciate what I can bring.

Another huge positive is Jill Ellis, Pia's assistant coach and my former U-21 coach. I have felt a special connection with Jill from the start. She is an authentic person, and I trust her completely. When she tells me something, I know it's motivated only by her desire to make me a better player.

She approaches me before a training session one day.

"When you are in the attacking third, you should keep doing what you are doing—taking people on, finding the right pass, getting yourself forward," Jill says. "You are an incredible weapon in that part of the field, but one area I think is important to concentrate on is your turnover-to-completion ratio in other parts of the field, when we are building up."

She goes on.

"A true, world-class center-mid should have a pass completion percentage in the mid to high eighties. When I look at your technical skills, I am thinking, *This player is so good —that's where she should be, not in the fifties or sixties.* This is all about making smart decisions and being conscious of ball security in our half of the field, getting us from the goalkeeper to the opponent's half. When you lose the ball there, it can put us in a dangerous situation. So it's good to be thinking about ball retention and not being wasteful. Make every possession count."

Pia is not into statistical analysis, but Jill is. During our training sessions, she keeps track of completion percentages.

When I come off, she'll tell me, "Sixty percent," or "Seventy percent." It becomes almost a game-within-a-game for us. I totally embrace the idea of taking greater care with every possession — learning when to take risks and when to keep it simple.

As a young player, I wanted to make an impression and often tried too hard to make a highlight-film play. Sometimes it would work. Other times the ball would get taken away. Like a young writer who reaches for big vocabulary words and elaborate constructions instead of something simple and direct, I am learning that less is more.

I am learning lots of things this year, probably as much as I have in my soccer career. During our training sessions when I'm home, James is encouraging me to connect more with my teammates and take advantage of what he calls "the togetherness factor." I keep to myself by nature, but during all the craziness of the Greg Ryan era and the World Cup, I withdrew even more. I wasn't sure where I fit in or what my future was, and it only heightened my natural insecurities.

Now things are different, and I need to respond accordingly. James and I agree that it's important for me to do less texting and more connecting, to ask questions and reach out to people more. I will be twenty-six by the time the Olympics come around. I am not the new kid anymore. It's quite clear that my spot on the team is not at all in jeopardy.

"Keep listening to the coaches and be supportive of all changes and subs they make," James writes to me in an email. "They fully support you, and you need to do the same. Your time has come to become a leader and lead this team into Olympic qualification and then lead them to Olympic gold."

Getting all this positive feedback makes me want to work even harder. I am grateful that I never have any issues with complacency. I sometimes can be my own worst enemy with my perfectionism, but the other side is that I am never satisfied. I never feel as though I've made it, so I keep working as if I am trying to make the team. I guess the pain from getting cut from South Jersey Select has stayed with me all these years.

I never want to feel that way again.

|||||

Returning home after the Algarve Cup, I take a few days off and then get right back into the Ark Road office. I do lots of ball work and drills with James and Ryan Finley, a fellow Universal Soccer Academy student and a U-18 national team player. We take turns serving crosses to each other. I work on finishing and taking free kicks. My routine includes regular ninety-minute runs, twelve 800-meter interval workouts, and punishing hill sprints in Laurel Acres Park. I also do lots of body-weight strength training, cranking out sets of push-ups and crunches, in addition to calf raises, squats, and work with resistance bands.

Every time I go home, my fitness goes to another level. It's as if I am a car just out of the shop, freshly tuned up, running leaner and stronger, more explosive off the line. Without Ark Road and James, none of this would be possible.

IIIII

We've qualified for the Olympics, and the opening ceremonies are not even two months away. I have started all fourteen games we've played under Pia, all of them victories. Things have never been better on the field, but the drama on Black Baron Drive in Delran doesn't want to let up.

Every time I'm home it feels as if I'm tiptoeing through a minefield. I never know when someone is going to go off. I'm doing better than I ever have with the national team, but the discord at home weighs on me constantly.

I make it a point not to spend too much time there when I am back on breaks. I stay with friends, and that becomes a point of contention too.

"I don't understand why you hardly ever have dinner with us and don't spend more time with your family after you've been away," my mother says.

The fact is that, even though I love my family, home is about the last place I want to be just now.

I return to Jersey for a few weeks before I begin final preparations for my first Olympic Games. I do not need any family drama.

One night when I am out, I call home and my father answers. He starts right in on me. I don't want to hear it.

"You never want to hear it," he says. "You never want to hear anything we have to say. Why don't you get over here and get your stuff out of the house, or I will throw it out the window?" I can't believe it's reached this point. But true to my stubborn self, I don't back down.

"If that's how you want it, fine," I say.

I drive over to the house, pull up in front, and take a breath. I step over the curb I used to spend hours kicking the ball against. I look at the side yard that was my field when I wasn't down at the park. Being nostalgic is not my natural inclination, but it's inevitable, given the circumstances.

I walk in the house and head straight upstairs. It's the saddest day of my life. I begin packing up all of my belongings. My mother and sister come into my room, and we all start crying. I am overwhelmed and so sad. I can't even believe this is happening.

When I'm finished, I head to Brian's mom's house, weeping as I drive. It feels so final, so crushing. I've lived my whole life in that house. Every minute of it. And now my own family doesn't want me anymore.

I get to Brian's mom's place and try to pull it together, but the tears keep coming. I am exhausted and utterly drained.

It takes a long time to fall asleep.

||||||

Days after I move out, I fly to South Korea with my teammates. The tournament is called the Peace Cup. Peace sounds very nice after all the tumult I've been through.

I am rooming with Shannon Boxx, and it's fun, the attacking and holding mids bonding between training sessions and ice baths. Maybe I shouldn't be surprised, given the events at home, but my body feels tapped out and my legs feel as if I'm wearing ankle weights.

Our first game in the Peace Cup is against Australia, and I am brutal. It's my worst game since we played Norway in the Algarve Cup. I give up the ball often and beat myself up each time I do.

Our next game is against Brazil, and I'm in a much better

Love at first kick.

I love the Phillies! Here's me (left) at old Veterans Stadium with my cousin Jaime Schoeffling Bula.

The Delran Dynamite helped get me on my way, thanks to my coach Karen Thornton and her assistant coach, Steve Lloyd, my dad.

Playing for the Medford Strikers was one of the best times in my soccer career.

Making the Olympic Development Program Region I team was a big deal for me at thirteen years old. I'm in the front row holding the plaque.

Family of five: the Lloyds of Delran. From left to right: my dad; my sister, Ashley; my brother, Stephen; me; and my mom.

Early years training with James Galanis.

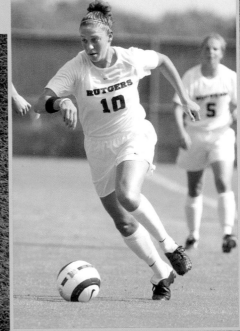

On the attack in my days with the Rutgers Scarlet Knights.

There's no such thing as a snow day when it comes to getting in my training.

My closest friends—Heather Mitts and Hope Solo—and I took a climb up the Great Wall of China before the Beijing Games.

My longtime teammate and fellow midfielder Shannon Boxx and I are all smiles before a game in the 2010 Algarve Cup in Portugal.

There's no sweeter feeling in soccer than scoring at a big moment. Here's the strike that beat Brazil in the 2008 Olympic gold medal game in Beijing. That's Formiga looking on.

My coach Pia Sundhage had open arms after I scored the game-winner against Brazil in Beijing.

My mom and dad behind me at right and most of our family gathered at the Philadelphia airport to celebrate after we won gold at the 2008 Olympics in Beijing.

We gave it our all against Japan in the 2011 World Cup final in Germany, a heartbreaking loss in PKs.

France, one of the best teams in the world, gave us a battle in the 2011 World Cup semifinals.

place mentally. I've forgotten about Australia and am treating this as a clean sheet, except that ten minutes in, I go up for a header and smack my nose into the back of somebody's head.

Blood starts gushing. I don't realize until the trainer and doctor come on the field that my nose is broken and on the side of my face. I get subbed out, and they take me into the locker room, where the doctor examines me. With no warning, he snaps my nose back into place.

The pain is way worse than when I smashed into the Brazilian player's head.

I get fitted with a hideous mask with a beak that sticks out about two inches and makes me look like a falcon. That is what we call the mask: the Falcon. I decorate it with a U.S. Soccer sticker and a Nike swoosh, but the artwork doesn't make it any less clunky.

We beat Brazil, 1–0, and I return to play the next game with the Falcon strapped on my face. I can't stand it. I play okay in a 2–0 victory over Italy, getting an assist on a corner kick, but in our final game against Canada, much stronger competition, I am not very good again. My passes are off and my touches are off, and I am not running the way I typically do. My frustration is getting the best of me. Pia subs me out at halftime. It is the right move to make.

Afterward, she talks to me.

"How can we handle this if this happens at the Olympics? I don't want to have to take you out. I want you to play every minute of every game. What do you think was going on to-night?"

"I think I just let the mask get in my head," I say. "I hate it. It's hard for me to see the ball and have clean touches. I wasn't playing well, and then I got down on myself when I made mis-takes."

I don't tell Pia this, but overcoming this penchant for self-criticism is still one of my biggest challenges as a player . . . giving myself permission to screw up and not let it put me into a downward spiral. James talks to me about it all the time. We have more work to do.

The best thing about the whole trip is the connection I forge with Boxxy. Even though we've played together for several years, this is the most time we've spent together. We butted heads somewhat when I first came on the team, but now we're in a completely different place. She's such a com-mitted, team-first player, doing tremendous work without a lot of fanfare. When you are on a team, at any level, you know who the people are who do the dirty work, who just keep putting out and giving, usually without much acclaim attached. That's Shannon Boxx. She centers me and supports me through all my struggles on this trip, and I am so thankful she is my roommate.

After a brief return home, we have a quick two-game series in Norway and Sweden. We crush Norway, 4–0, and beat Sweden, 1–0. I have ditched the Falcon in favor of a new custom mask, which is far more streamlined and manageable. I can actually play with it. I score in both matches and am back on my game, especially against Sweden.

Now there are only two games left before we leave for China and the Olympics—both against Brazil. We're 19–0–1 under Pia and an entirely different team from the one that showed up in that disastrous World Cup semifinal nine months earlier. We beat Brazil, 1–0, in Commerce City, Colorado, and head west to San Diego. Our final game before the Olympics is on my twenty-sixth birthday—July 16.

Just over thirty minutes in, the ball is loose and bouncing near the top of the box. Abby is gunning for it, and so is a Brazilian defender named Andreia Rosa. They collide violently. Abby goes down.

She goes down hard.

Oh no, I am thinking. *Abby, please get up.*

Abby does not get up. She motions for medical attention.

This is bad, I am thinking.

Unfortunately, I am not wrong. Abby Wambach, our leading scorer for the year with thirteen goals and ten assists, a player who is on her way to being the most prolific scorer in U.S. Soccer history, has broken her leg in two places. When the trainers ask if she can move her leg, she says, "It's broken."

It is a grotesque sight, and it is unthinkable. This is Abby. She is as close to indestructible as any athlete I know. The Olympics are twenty days away.

Can this really be happening?

It is a horrific, sickening reminder of how fragile our world is. One minute you are one of the top goal-scorers on earth, and the next you are a hospital case.

There is a record crowd of more than 7,500 in Torero Stadium, and almost all of them are quiet. They celebrate in the eighty-fifth minute when Natasha Kai heads in my free kick for the only goal of the game, but who is kidding whom?

We just lost Abby Wambach three weeks before the Olympics. There is nothing at all to celebrate.

"Abby is a great player," Pia tells the press, "but it's not about one player, it's about the team. Still, we will miss her —Abby is Abby. We'll have to change a little bit."

Hope Solo, firmly entrenched once more in goal, insists there is too much character on our team for us to quit now and says, "We're a winning team, and we're going to find a way to win."

Abby says, "Above everything else, I'm only one player, and you can never win a championship with just one player. I have the utmost confidence in this team bringing home the gold."

The memory of our painful and awkward conversation at the end of the World Cup is long gone. A great athlete and teammate is badly injured. I watch her getting carted off the field, and all I feel is deep compassion for the great Abby Wambach.

9

FINE CHINA

OUR BRAVE FACE ABOUT LIFE without Abby lasts about the time it takes to sing the national anthem. We open the Olympics against Norway, a team we've outscored 12–1 in our last three meetings, in the coastal town of Qinhuangdao, about 200 miles east of Beijing. It is a summer resort area noted for its invigorating breezes and prime bird watching. In the second minute, there is not a bird in sight—only the ball in the back of the U.S. goal. Hope had come off her line, leaping to punch out a long ball, but ended up colliding violently with Lori Chalupny instead. Both of them went sprawling. A Norwegian winger named Leni Kaurin took advantage of the miscommunication and headed the ball into the empty net.

Wait. It gets worse.

In the third minute, defender Kate Markgraf knocks a backpass toward Christie Pearce Rampone, but it is too soft, too slow. Before Rampone gets near it, Norway's Melissa Wiik swoops in and tucks the ball just inside the left post.

We are 180 seconds into the Olympics, and we are down two goals. I'd expect the Great Wall to crumble before I'd expect us to open our Games this way. We never recover and lose 2–0. Norway is the only team other than the U.S. to win Olympic gold — the Norwegians won in Sydney in 2000 — so it's not as if they can't play. But come on, how can this be happening?

It is the first time the U.S. has ever lost in group play in the Olympics. Already the media is sounding the refrain that we can't win without Abby. I am not quite sure how the Olympic setup works, but I think our medal hopes might already be history until Pia explains that we can still advance to the elimination round if we win our next two games. Later that night, Pia asks Christie, Boxxy, and me to come see her in her hotel room.

"You are the core of this team," she says. "You are the ones who have to help us regroup and get the team going. We need a quick attitude change. We can't do anything about Norway. We've got a tough game against Japan in three days, and everything from here on has to be positive. I believe in this team as much as ever, but you are the ones who have to set the tone on the field."

It is a great meeting, and a pivotal message.

Japan is a technically skilled team. They like to carve you up with a tiki-taka possession game. We are not at our best still, but we battle hard and play with commitment and urgency. In the twenty-seventh minute of the first half, our defender, Stephanie Cox, controls the ball near the Japanese end line, gets some space, and sends a cross toward the 18-yard line. I see what's coming and run onto it and belt a volley that dives just below the crossbar into the Japanese goal. We've finally joined the Olympic party.

Our next stop is in Shenyang, a 2,000-year-old city in northeast China, not that far from Inner Mongolia. Our opponent is New Zealand. A victory could lock up our group for us, provided that the Norwegians lose to Japan. We deliver a powerful, high-energy performance, winning 4–0. We advance to the quarterfinals against Canada, thanks to the Japanese, who cooperate by beating Norway.

The Canadians have beaten us in only three of our forty-three matches, but the gap is narrowing. We won a hard-fought, 1–0 game in our most recent meeting in the South Korea Peace Cup. With Christine Sinclair, one of the world's premier goal-scorers, on their side, there isn't anybody thinking this game will be easy when it kicks off in Shanghai.

Angela Hucles scores to give us the lead in the first half.

Then the skies open up, and it starts to pour. Lightning bolts flash all around the stadium, as if the whole sky is plugged in. Play is stopped for ninety minutes, and we return to the locker room to wait it out. Some people stretch, and others sing or play games. I am content to sit quietly and get geared up mentally for the rest of the game.

When the game resumes, Sinclair ties it up with a missile just beyond a diving Hope's reach. A taut game heads into overtime; then finally, eleven minutes in, forward Natasha Kai converts a diving header, Abby-style. Tasha is immediately swarmed. A soggy and wildly happy celebration spills everywhere.

Into the semifinals we go, in Workers Stadium in Beijing, a half-century-old concrete oval in the northeast section of the city. It's a world apart from the gleaming, new-age venues in Olympic Park.

Our opponent is Japan again, and they are in a confident, attacking mindset from the start. Hope parries away a threat in the opening minute, before a defensive lapse leaves an unmarked player in front on a corner kick. Hope has no chance, and we are down 1–0. It stays that way until the closing minutes of the half, when Heather O'Reilly has one of her signature high-speed bursts down the right flank. She crosses in front to Hucles, who slots in a left-footer to tie the game.

In the forty-fourth minute, Markgraf finds me with a good ball near the center line. I shield the defender, take two touches, and send it ahead to Amy Rodriguez. Amy quickly finds Lori Chalupny, who eludes a defender on the left, cuts in front, and fires a shot under heavy pressure into the upper left corner. We're up a goal and on our way to a 4–2 victory and another shot at Brazil, the team that stomped on us right here in China eleven months before.

The Brazilians advance with a shocking 4–1 rout of Germany in the other semifinal, a reversal of the World Cup final result. Now we have a reversal of our own in mind, and nobody wants it more than Hope. She started the whole mess last year with her comments about how she believed she would've made a difference in the final against Brazil at the World Cup.

Now she's got the chance she wanted. Let's see if she can prove her point. No, it's not a World Cup final, but it's the next best thing.

I prepare with a careful reading of James's latest email. For years he has emailed me before major competitions. His words aren't just sustenance; they are my motivational rocket fuel.

He begins:

Ms. Lloyd,

Wow, you are in the final of the Olympics. It's been an amaz-

ing run thus far. Over the last five games you have grown as a
player more than I imagined. You have gone from a player who
works hard but wastes energy to a player who works hard and
saves the energy for the right moments. Your play in midfield
has more than helped your team get to this point.

After a game-by-game evaluation of my performance during the Olympics, James closes with two final points:

Your Chance to be the Biggest

Keep your head up high. With a little more work and a little
more concentration you can steal the show and wake the world
to who you are. You need to focus on being steady and taking
advantage of your chances. I know you will get chances and you
need to make them count. Two goals or an MVP performance will
set you up as a top-5 player in the world, just in time [to be] the
top player at the next Olympics.

The Game

This game is big to the world of soccer. However, you need
to go in and treat it like another game. That's what you do best.
Work the hardest, concentrate the most and be ready for any-
thing. Don't give up and let it all out (empty the tank). I really feel
that you are going to win because you're a better TEAM. They are
individuals. Teams always beat individuals. But if you don't win
just make sure the Brazilians feel like they went through a tor-

ture chamber to get the win. Don't give it to them easy. Pressure them and fight them to the end. Right now the GOLD is in your hands. Only the Brazilians can take it off you. If you let them.

James Galanis

|||||

From the start, it's clear that Marta and Cristiane, the dynamic stars of the Brazilian side, are bringing all they've got, and so is Hope Solo. I've seen Hope play lots of great games. I've never seen her more confident or sharper than she is tonight, on a rain-slickened field with humidity that makes the air feel like oatmeal.

At her best, Marta is a magician in a canary-yellow shirt, making the ball appear Velcroed to her foot. So it is in this epic game. In the seventy-second minute, she runs down a ball to the left of our goal, eludes Heather Mitts and Kate Markgraf, and blasts a left-footed shot toward the near post from point-blank range. Hope dives left but raises her right arm as she does, as if she were a traffic cop, stopping traffic. The ball slams into her right arm and ricochets away.

Marta, World Player of the Year about a hundred times, cannot believe it. She buries her face in her hands.

It's the save of the tournament, the year—probably one of the greatest saves in Olympic history. It gives us an incredible lift. All game, Hope is snaring crosses in traffic, punching away threats.

We have our best chance in the ninetieth minute, when Amy Rodriguez gets in behind the Brazilian defense with only Barbara, the Brazil keeper, left to beat. Barbara charges out and Amy tries to chip it over her, but Barbara grabs it easily.

The back-and-forth chances, the drama, keep building, and now the game goes into two fifteen-minute overtimes, Brazil looking for its first major championship, the U.S. looking for its third Olympic gold in four tries. All I can think as overtime begins is:

This is why I train. This is why I run those hills in Laurel Acres, do those eight hundred repeats, the ninety-minute distance runs. It's why I do all the body-weight exercises, why James and I keep pushing for more and better ways to get me fitter. I empty the tank in training so the tank is never empty in games.

We are in Brazil's end, six minutes into overtime, when Lauren Cheney, who had come on for Lindsay Tarpley, slips a short pass to me. I hold off a defender and backheel a ball to Amy, who takes a touch and threads it back to me under heavy pressure. I see a sliver of space and explode forward, take a touch, and let fly with my left foot. The ball shoots low and hard, a skidding one-hopper heading toward the right corner. Barbara dives to her left.

She might get a fingernail on the ball. She cannot stop it. The ball is in the Brazilian goal, and I am running toward my teammates, arms pumping, joy pouring from me as I hug Boxxy first and then everybody else. I run over and hug Pia. She is the one who believed in me, who started me every game this whole year and wanted me to be the hub of the U.S. attack.

|||||

There are still twenty-four minutes to play, and Brazil keeps the pressure on. Marta does a pullback move, spins left, and rips a shot just over the crossbar. The pressure on the defense and Hope is constant. In a counterattack in the final minutes, I get behind the defense and spank another left-footer, this one thudding off the far post.

Brazil still has life. The clock is crawling; every second feels as if it's taking ten seconds. Brazil has three straight corners at the end of the game. Marta's inswinging ball finds Renata Costa near the far post, but her header hits the outside of the netting. On a final chance, Costa arches the ball in the box to Cristiane, who drives a low header that Hope stops.

The whistle blows. We are jumping, screaming, crying, embracing. Nobody thought we could ever win without Abby, and now we've done it.

Hope runs out of the goal and wraps me in her arms, and neither of us has to say a word about the sweetness of this ending — Cup outcasts turned Olympic heroes. We are a team again, all in it together, fighting for each other, sacrificing for each other, with lots of perseverance and perspiration, not drama or dissent. It is a total team triumph, from Angela Hucles, our leading scorer up top, to Heather Mitts and the rest of our relentless defenders in the back, and Hope's all-world effort in the net. You can't single anybody out. We've all given everything we've got, for 120 minutes, the contributions coming from everywhere. If Lauren Cheney doesn't slip me a deft pass with the outside of her foot seconds before the game-winner, if Amy Rodriguez doesn't hold off two defenders and find me on a give-and-go, there is no gold-medal-winning goal.

That's the beauty of soccer: so many little moves have to be made, so many little battles have to be won, to produce the ultimate victory. Our joy, a feeling that is as pure and good as the gold medal itself, is well earned and shared by everyone.

Later that night, our team liaison in Beijing, a young Chinese woman whose nickname is Bean Bean, takes us to a private party. David Beckham is there, and I get to talk to him. The actor Vince Vaughn is there too. I get a photo with both of them. My gold medal is around my neck. It stays there for a long time.

|||||

A week after I return home, a parade is held in Delran in my honor, complete with the high school marching band, the Knights of Columbus, the VFW, and most every fire truck, police car, and EMS vehicle in town, along with hundreds of little kids in their soccer uniforms. My old coaches, Joe Dadura from the Strikers, Rudi Klobach from Delran High, and Glenn Crooks from Rutgers, are there too. It is Labor Day. The parade starts at Vermes Field, where I used to play, and heads down Tenby Chase Road to Conrow Road to the high school. I ride in the top of a fire truck, wearing a black dress and a gold medal, and wave until my arm hurts. My parents are also waving, in the back of a red convertible.

The day winds up with a ceremony on the football field, where a bunch of politicians give speeches and everybody talks about me. My parents and brother and sister are all sitting on the stage, a penalty kick away from Brian and me.

I don't tell anybody about getting booted out of my own

house right before the Olympics. It would kind of spoil the moment.

From start to finish, the event is a sweet, small-town tribute. I appreciate the sentiment and being able to share the Olympic achievement with so many people who have been there for me along the way. But the truth is that I don't like being fussed over, and never have. I'm way more comfortable practicing volleys on Ark Road than listening to people celebrate me and tell me how great I am. I never want to be rude to anyone, but I am a person who likes her inner circle small and her gatherings intimate.

I try to explain this to my parents when they begin to plan a post-parade party at the house.

"I know you want to include a lot of people and make it a big celebration, but I'd really prefer to have it just be close family and friends, since I don't see them very often," I tell my mother.

"Carli, so many people have shared in this and want to be a part of it. We can't not include them," my mother says.

I don't want to start more dramas, so I don't carry it much further.

More than anything, I want the strife to go away and to be able to enjoy this time with my parents, brother, and sister. This is not how I want to go through my life, exiled from my own flesh and blood, people I love and have spent my whole life with.

Things seem to be improving a bit as the fall arrives. I sort of move back in, staying at home occasionally, but the friction is always quick to flare back up.

I realize I need to be out of the house for good, and I start looking for a place to buy. I find a nice townhome with a fireplace and a clean, airy feel about it. I make a couple of trips back to my parents' house to collect a few last items.

Three months after the exhilarating run at the Olympics, it's clear to me that my relationship with my parents is at an all-time low. I spend the first Thanksgiving of my life away from them. I am with Brian and his family, and I love them, but I still have so much sadness.

As Christmas approaches, I email my parents because I need some photos of me when I was young and they have my photo albums. I tell them they can leave them on the porch and I will pick them up.

Nobody is home when I arrive. I walk up to the porch and see several big boxes of my things. My father has packed up my stuff and left it for me. In one of the boxes are the scrapbooks and binders he meticulously kept from the very beginning of my soccer career. Newspaper clippings, press releases, tournament results, awards.

Everything.

Next to the bags is a card and my Christmas gift, a set of pots and pans for my new home. I drop off my gift for them —a gift certificate to the Cheesecake Factory—and lug the boxes to my car. I leave the pots and pans behind.

10

LETTING GO OF GOLD

JAMES IS CONCERNED ABOUT ME, probably more concerned than he has been in almost five years of working together. It's not so much the family drama as it is how I look in training at the end of 2008 and early in 2009. I am putting in the time, training hard. But James doesn't see the same intensity, the I'll-prove-them-wrong edge that has driven me for so long.

"You are not training at full capacity. You're not as mentally engaged as you need to be," James says. "You've got to train harder and be fully committed mentally."

I get a little defensive. It hasn't happened often in my time with James, but he has never questioned my commitment before.

Not once.

"What do you mean, train harder? I'm here. I'm doing the work. I don't think I'm slacking off."

More than anyone I've ever met, James Galanis finds a way to be supportive and tough all at once. At times he will criticize me pointedly, and I still feel as if I've gotten a hug. That is not easy to pull off.

"You are doing the work, Carli, yes," James says. "But it's not the same way as you've always trained. I am watching closely, and I see a difference. I need you to get back to being the underdog."

I wish I could say he is wrong, but he's not. James knows exactly what the issue is, and so do I. It's the Beijing afterglow. Suddenly, for the first time since making the national team, I am the flavor-of-the-day, getting attention that usually goes to Abby or Hope or Aly Wagner, which went to Mia Hamm and Julie Foudy and Kristine Lilly before that. I am named U.S. Soccer's Player of the Year. I don't think it goes to my head. I don't want it to go to my head. But when you're being celebrated as never before, it's natural to stop and think, *I guess I am pretty good.*

James goes right after it, treating these nascent complacent thoughts as if they were a pack of termites ready to chew through the foundation we've worked so hard to build. He is happy to play the role of exterminator. He begins by scribbling a message on a little chalkboard in his basement, where I do off-season strength and fitness training.

The sign reads:

THE OLYMPICS ARE FORGOTTEN

James does everything but brand the words into my brain. It's good that he does.

Things are a struggle for me from the outset of 2009. I am on fire in our first camp of the year in January, feeling fit and playing in top form, certain that I've put the afterglow issue behind me. I lose my sharpness as camp goes on. Pia notices, of course.

"I don't want you to lose your drive to be the best," she says. "You have to stay switched on through every single training session."

"I know you're right," I say. "I haven't felt challenged. I've been kind of bored. I know I have to step it up."

Camp finishes on a much better note, but there are number of new players in the mix, especially in the midfield. We don't play our best in our annual visit to Portugal for the Algarve Cup, falling to Sweden on PKs in the final. Abby is still not quite back from her broken leg from the previous summer, and with another World Cup still two years away, it's a low-key year for the national team.

My main focus is on my new team, the Chicago Red Stars, of Women's Professional Soccer (WPS). I am one of the marquee players on the team, along with Lindsay Tarpley, Brazil's

Cristiane, and Megan Rapinoe, but it turns into a season-long nightmare, as we never really mesh and win only one of our first nine games. I wind up playing a good deal of forward and score just two goals in twenty games.

I feel out of my element almost the whole season. We finish 5-10-5 and don't make the playoffs. I book out of Chicago in early August and head for the Jersey Shore.

After a few days off, I get back to training with James. It's just what I need to put a frustrating season behind me. I have started to make big changes in my diet, cutting out candy and sugar and almost all carbs. I feel leaner and better already. It's all good, until my phone rings one day. I am at home in my bedroom. I've just finished a monster workout with James. The caller is Pia Sundhage.

"Carli, I want to give you a heads-up before the official email goes out," she says. "You don't have a renewed contract [with U.S. Soccer] for 2009." (Twice a year we get renewed, not renewed, or bumped down a tier.) "If you do get a contract, it may not be Tier I [the top pay scale]."

I am stunned. I know I didn't have a great season in Chicago, but not to be renewed by a coach who told me she thought I could be one of the best players in the world?

I am on the verge of a meltdown, but I try not to give that away.

"Okay. Can I ask why?"

"Well, you weren't in your best form early in the year, and then the WPS season didn't go the way you or I were figuring it would either. The consensus is that, for whatever reason, you are not the same impact player you were.

"Now, what happens from here is up to you. You will have plenty of chances in September, October, and December to show that you have improved your game and get your contract, but I wanted to let you know."

I hang up the phone and think I am going to throw up. I am livid. I am sick. It feels as if my world is crashing all around me, my brain stuck on a nasty and self-critical refrain:

How could I have screwed this up? How could this be happening? A year ago I was a gold medal hero and the Player of the Year, and now U.S. Soccer doesn't want to renew my contract. Can anybody tell me how it has gotten to this point?

As angry as I am, as much as I might want to blame somebody or beat myself up, I know this is no time for self-pity. It is time to go to work as I never have before.

Without delay, James and I launch into two-a-day sessions, determined to pound me into the greatest shape I have ever been in. I run distance. Run sprints. Run hills, and run through drills. I am sore and miserable and exhausted, mentally and physically, as I push beyond thresholds I've never crossed before. But the hurt is accompanied by empowerment.

I am in the best condition of my life. I don't think it. I know it. Between the workouts and the changes in my diet, my confidence picks up. I am anxious about the upcoming camp. I also am determined to kick butt and show Pia how wrong it was not to renew me.

The underdog is back in a big way.

Before I leave for camp, James emails to say how proud he is that I did all the work without complaining.

"You are going to not only get a contract but also take over the WNT," he says. "Don't worry. Just keep working. We are all in. No other way."

Camp starts at the training center in Carson, California, on September 21 and goes for twelve days. From the time I step on the field, I am as sharp and confident as I've been in months. My mind is completely clear, unburdened by doubt or complication.

After the Olympics, I felt I had to meet all the expectations people had—had to make magic happen on each possession. So instead of playing simply, naturally, I would sometimes force things and take needless risks. Nothing messes you up on a soccer field more than that.

Now I am free of that thinking, and the difference is striking. Pia comes up to me after day two of camp.

"You are looking very fit, very good," she says. "It's good to see you back in top form."

"I don't want to go backwards again," I say. "I'm hitting the delete button on last season. It's a fresh start, and I feel like I'm ready to crush it."

A few days later, I am leaving breakfast and I run into Pia again. She asks if we can talk.

"When I look at you now compared with the player I saw in the Algarve and in the WPS, the difference is truly night and day. How did this happen? It would help me to know how you did it."

"It's pretty simple, Pia. I worked harder than I ever have in my life, so now I feel fit and confident. I think that is what you are seeing." I remind her of what I've told Greg and Jill and other coaches I've worked with through the years: a high level of fitness doesn't come easily to me. Some players can do minimal training and go hard for ninety minutes. That is not me. When I do all the extra stuff that I need to do, it changes everything.

"Well, I am very happy for you," Pia says. "You've shown

me so much and you deserve your contract, so we will get that done."

I wind up getting traded to the Jersey team in WPS, Sky Blue FC, and that is more good news, because I get to be near home. There has been no thaw with my parents, but otherwise I am in a much better place than I was a few months ago. James doesn't tell me this at the time, but he thinks getting knocked on my can is exactly what I needed.

||||||

The 2010 season gets off to the best start. We finish a strong Algarve Cup with a 3–2 victory over Germany.

"That's the greatest game I've ever seen you play. You looked so fit, and you owned the middle of the field," Pia says.

After a miserable Women's Professional Soccer season with Chicago in 2009, I can't wait to get going for Sky Blue.

We split our first two games, and I'm not altogether thrilled with my performance, but about a third of the way through our third game — against my old team, the Red Stars — I'm back in prime form. I'm playing holding mid because my teammate, Yael Averbuch, is out sick. I am tackling well, winning balls, changing the point of attack, and spraying the ball out wide. Then, in the twenty-seventh minute, I play a ball to Natasha Kai, and as I do, I lose my footing, all of my weight goes on my left leg, and my left ankle buckles like a cheap chair. I hear the crack.

I lie on the field for a few moments and then walk off on my own. I want to tape it up and go back in, but the trainer says it doesn't look right, and the team doctor believes it is broken. I go to the emergency room at halftime, and the X-rays confirm that I have a broken fibula.

I get a cast for two weeks, and then a boot. I start jogging at six weeks, at the team's urging. It is way too much, way too soon. It still hurts, and I have to back off until I attend the national team camp in July. Even then I am not right, and I mostly work out on the side. Finally, I start to train in late August and into September, and I get back on the field with the national team at the next training camp, in late September.

I make my first start for the U.S. since March on October 2 against China. It seems as if it's been ten times that long. I am anxious about being back out there, but I play simply and effectively, going for understatement rather than flash. Then we are off to Cancun, Mexico, for World Cup qualifying.

Before the games start, Pia meets with me and underscores how much the team needs me to step up, especially in the attacking third.

"You have all the tools in the world and can be the best, and that's what we need," she says.

"I know I can get more fit. That's what I want too," I say.

We breeze through games against Haiti and Guatemala — I am named Player of the Match in both — but then we look only so-so in a 4–0 victory over Costa Rica before we play the host team, Mexico, in the CONCACAF semifinals.

In front of 8,000 fans in a boisterous, sold-out stadium, we pick a horrible time for a letdown. We give up a goal in the opening minutes, which makes the crowd even louder. I tie it up, winning a scramble in front after a Megan Rapinoe cross, in the twenty-fifth minute, but the Mexicans answer right back with another score. We are totally out of sync, playing kickball, and even though we outshoot Mexico, 10–1, in the second half, the score does not change.

I am angry and in complete disbelief at our collective level of play. Mexico took it to us, and we allowed our nerves to make us tentative and inconsistent, an effort that made U.S. Soccer history: the first loss to the Mexican women in twenty-six matches.

Now we are in a major fix. We have to beat Costa Rica for third place and then beat Italy, just to qualify for the World Cup. Everybody figured we'd waltz through qualifying.

Maybe that was the problem. We have a team meeting, and I bring up the disastrous game against Norway to start the 2008 Olympics.

"We have to be more of a team. We can't just think that because it says USA on our jerseys, teams are going to lie down for us," I say.

We are better in a 3–0 victory against Costa Rica, and then we head to Italy right before Thanksgiving for our biggest game since the 2008 Olympics.

Playing in the ancient northern Italian city of Padua, we generate tons of chances and are playing well, but not finishing. I am so fresh and energized that I feel as if I could run to Rome and back. I am all over the field. In extra time, I ping a long ball to Abby, who flicks it to Alex Morgan, a new kid with great speed and a knack for scoring big goals, and she finishes it. We win, 1–0, and head back to the States for a return match with Italy in Bridgeview, Illinois.

We have a series of meetings and a film breakdown. Before one of the meetings, the team has a ceremony in honor of my one hundredth cap, a milestone I will reach in this next game. Paul Rogers, our goalkeeper coach, shows a video of me in action. Christie, our captain, gets up and addresses all of us.

"This is a great achievement and well deserved," Christie

says. "Carli, I've seen you grow so much from your college days at Rutgers until now. Your dedication and hard work are unmatched, and mentally you are so strong. You are someone who never quits and never backs off, and that's how you've gotten to this point."

Everybody applauds. There is a slide show of pictures of me through the years, and a framed USWNT jersey with number 100 on it is presented to me. Later, I receive a Rolex from U.S. Soccer, which I upgrade with an engraving that says:

100TH CAP
ITALY
NOVEMBER 27, 2010

It is a happy day all around, even though we play a sloppy game, winning 1–0 on a goal by Amy Rodriguez. The only thing that matters is that we have qualified for the World Cup in Germany next summer and have averted the unthinkable.

I stick around Chicago for a day to watch the Eagles lose to the Chicago Bears, and then I go into a six-week break with my ankle almost completely healed and my head in a good place. I can't wait to be back in my home.

After giving my body a little time to recharge, I dive back into phase 2 of James's training, the goal being to further establish myself as a core player with the national team. The training begins with a series of long runs to build up my aerobic base, finishing with the prescribed ninety-minute runs. I run in the snow and cold. I layer up and go. I mix in indoor training twice a week, and then I start up with track workouts, doing 800-meter repeats on some days and twenty-five sprints up the Laurel Acres hill on others.

To mix it up, I get in the car and drive twenty miles west, across the Walt Whitman Bridge into Philadelphia. I turn onto Benjamin Franklin Parkway and head toward the Philadelphia Museum of Art, home to the steps made famous by Sylvester Stallone/Rocky Balboa on the big screen. There are seventy-two steps in front of the museum. Sometimes I take them one at a time, other times two at a time. I have never stepped foot inside the museum, only on the concrete leading up to it. I run Rocky's steps thirty-five times. Nobody is singing, "getting strong now" in the background, but that is exactly what I am doing.

11

EMPTY CUP

JAMES GALANIS IS MY GREATEST supporter, but Pia Sundhage is not far behind. All year in the run-up to my second go at the World Cup, Pia tells me that she wants me in attack mode, wants me to be the focal point of everything. The day she announces our Cup roster—it includes twelve first-timers—Pia tells me that the whole key for us is for me to get forward as much as possible and to have Shannon Boxx taking care of things as the defensive midfielder.

I love Pia's faith; it couldn't be any more different from life under Greg Ryan, who treated me as if I were radioactive at the end of the 2007 World Cup. But sometimes my game to-do list seems overly ambitious. Pia wants me to be the playmaker, make runs behind the forward line, switch the point of attack, distribute the ball around the field, key our possession game, and tackle and win balls on the defensive end.

A month before the World Cup, we have two games against Japan. Before the second one, in Cary, North Carolina, I speak to Pia. I feel as if she thinks I am wearing a cape and a big *S* for Superwoman. I am frustrated, and Pia can see it.

"What do you need from me?" she asks.

"I'm thinking too much out there about everything you want me to do," I reply. "I'm not playing freely, and it's affecting my confidence. I'm much better when I can just play."

Pia hears me, but I know that she is feeling enormous pressure. She's led us to Olympic gold, but this is the ultimate prize — what we've been working for ever since we crashed out against Brazil four years earlier.

This is why she was hired.

We're the number-one-ranked team in the world, but we've had our bumps along the way, for sure. After surviving the qualifying scare, we lost our first game of the year to Sweden and followed a stellar Algarve Cup with our first loss to England since 1988.

We seem much better for having gone through all that. We win the two games against Japan, then beat Mexico, 1–0, in our sendoff game in New Jersey. We fly to Salzburg, Austria, for our final training sessions before we travel to Dresden to play North Korea in our first group game. Brian, Aunt Patti,

Uncle Wayne, and Jaime are there. So are Jaime's husband, Alex, and his brother, Andre. Though I'm grateful for their love and support, I'm concerned that they could be a distraction if I am worrying about their tickets and how they're doing. I do not want to be distracted. It happened four years ago in China, and we know how that played out.

I am nervous as the North Korea game begins, but I ease my way into it and get tons of work done. I possess the ball effectively and make some nice passes, one of them a long, left-footed pass to Abby, who swings out to the left flank and crosses it in to Lauren Cheney. Lauren heads it in for our first score of the tournament. Rachel Buehler drills home our second goal and we win, 2–0.

Next we knock off Colombia, 3–0. One of the highlights is a missile of a strike outside the box by Heather O'Reilly. Megan Rapinoe follows with a wonderful hustle play. After throwing the ball in, she sprints toward the box and finishes with a superb strike of her own. And I get my first World Cup goal to wrap up the scoring.

Then it's on to the city of Wolfsburg, where we play Sweden. We're assured of advancing out of our group, and all we need to do is tie Sweden to avoid a quarterfinal against Brazil.

Every tournament, and every year, has its own narrative, and this year's seems to be that we refuse to do things the easy way. Sweden is a physical team that always plays us tough, and since our coach is an iconic Swedish player, that goes double this time around. The Swedes convert an early PK and score a freakish second goal when a direct kick caroms off of Amy LePeilbet's thigh into the goal. We lose, 2–1, the first time the U.S. women have ever lost a group-stage game. Sweden wins our group, and we get Brazil, as tough a quarterfinal as you could ever have, back in Dresden.

I am not terribly stressed about having to play Brazil, honestly. The way I see it, we owe them for what happened four years ago. They are staying in the same hotel as us, and wherever they seem to go, their fans like to pound on drums and break into song, as if they were on the beach in Rio during Carnival. It's part of their culture; I understand that. But I don't have to like it.

I don't have to do anything to work up an edge about the Brazilians.

We score on an own goal off a superb cross by Boxxy in the second minute, and then the U.S. and Brazil go at it in a two-hour quarterfinal crucible, a game with little rhythm, lots of tension, and more twists and turns than an amusement park ride. In the sixty-fifth minute, Marta flicks the ball to herself, bores in on Hope, and gets blocked by Rachel Buehler, who is sent off with a red card. Now we have to play a man down the rest of the way. Hope makes a spectacular diving stop of the PK by Cristiane, my old Red Stars teammate. It's an exhilarating turn of events, until the referee gives Brazil a rekick, apparently because Christie Rampone came in the box too soon. Marta converts the do-over to tie the game.

We press on, and the game goes into overtime. Marta scores again with a looping left-footed volley over Hope's outstretched arm. Outmanned and almost out of time, we desperately push to keep our World Cup alive but are generating few threats. Abby gets the ball in the box but is denied as she turns to shoot. I have a good look from twenty yards out, but I launch it over the crossbar in the 121st minute. We might get one more chance, if we are lucky. Cristiane gets the ball in the left corner and holds the ball against Christie, dawdling, hoping for the whistle. Christie finally gets a piece of it, and Ali Krieger runs onto the loose ball and sends it to me in the middle. I take three touches up the middle of the field and slide it over to Rapinoe on the left flank. The whistle is going to blow any second.

Quick, Pinoe, let it fly, I think.

Pinoe does exactly that, launching a long cross to the far post. Abby is in the neighborhood, tracking it, timing it. She is closely marked. She goes up. Andreia, the Brazilian keeper, bounds off her line and goes up to punch it away. Defender

Renata Costa, trying to get a body on Abby, goes up too. Abby gets to the ball first, though, snaps her head forward, and powers the ball into the near corner of the goal.

As the stadium erupts, Abby runs off to the corner and skids to her knees. It is the latest goal ever scored in the history of the Women's World Cup. It is about a million-to-one shot to tie the game the way we did, when we did.

Marta looks like she's just been hit with a plank. Who can blame her? Pia huddles us up, and Paul Rogers, the goalkeeper coach, chooses who will take the PKs and arranges the order. Paul works with us on PKs most every day after practice and keeps track of our success rate. I am so ready. I can't imagine any way we can lose after Abby's miracle header.

Boxxy buries the first PK. I step up and do the same, and when Hope makes a stunning stop with an all-out dive to her left, we have the sliver of an opening we need. Ali Krieger finishes it off with a low shot just an inch or two inside the left post, and the party is on. Suddenly a team that was about to pack up and head home and get ripped for another World Cup disappointment has become America's soccer sweethearts.

Funny how that goes.

I am up until all hours and can barely sleep. We meet the next day, and obviously the first task is to put Brazil behind us and get ready for a semifinal against France in Moncheng-gladbach, a city in western Germany.

Again we get off to an auspicious start. In the ninth minute, I backheel a ball up the sideline to Heather O'Reilly, who flashes down the flank and fires a cross that Lauren Cheney redirects for a dazzling finish. We don't sustain any momentum, though, and France dices us up with their technical skill and quick passing game. They completely dominate the half, even if the scoreboard shows us with the lead.

The French square the game at one about ten minutes into the second half, which I start, almost inexplicably, with three giveaways in midfield. I haven't been off the field the whole tournament, but I come off now. Pia subs me for Pinoe and moves Lauren Cheney into center midfield. I feel awful about this poor patch of play and am distraught that Pia wants me off the field. I feel as though I've let everybody down, and my old demons fire up like a blowtorch. I start feeling bad about my whole World Cup. Pinoe is electric, making things happen right away, and we seal a 3–1 victory. That's the most important thing. But even as we celebrate, I am trying to fight off a funk.

Pia tells me to stay positive and think about keeping things simple and keeping possession when we play the final against

Japan. They beat home team Germany and then Sweden to make it to their first World Cup final.

"You have to let go of this and start preparing mentally for the final," James says. "I'm glad this happened now, and glad you got to rest a little because you are going to be fresh and you're going to play your best game of the tournament when it matters the most."

He, too, talks about keeping it simple, making good decisions, and not trying to produce a highlight-film play with each touch.

"Just be Carli," he says. James reminds me of his key points in the usual email he sends before big matches. This final isn't just big. It's massive, the most important game of my career.

At a final run-through before we play Japan, Hege Riise, Pia's assistant coach, approaches me during stretching.

"I am so excited for you in this game," she says. "You always come up big in finals. I know this is going to be your time to shine."

"Thanks, Hege. I want nothing more than to shine and bring this World Cup back to the States."

On July 12, 2011, in Frankfurt, Germany, I am more nervous than I've ever been before a game. I have put France behind me, and I'm focusing completely on the next ninety minutes and heeding James's words.

Unlike so many other games this year, and in this tournament, we come out flying and make good on Pia's request to do better with possession. In the first minute, Lauren Cheney gets behind the defense and just misses giving us an insanely quick lead. We are buzzing the Japanese goal like hornets, connecting passes, possessing the ball better than we ever have. The ball zips cleanly from player to player, creating all kinds of chances against a side that normally does this sort of dictating. Abby has a great look but can't finish it. I get off a couple of dangerous shots but do not convert. Pinoe has a couple of prime chances, and Lauren has another one, but despite our domination, we cannot get on the board in the opening forty-five minutes.

I'm frustrated that we haven't broken through, but I feel so much better about my form and our collective level of play. Japan is about as skillful a team as there is in the world, and for half of a World Cup final, they are pretty much chasing us.

Keep on pushing. Keep on playing the same way, I tell myself. *It will come.*

And at last, in the sixty-ninth minute, it does. I am in a scrum near our 18-yard line, and I poke-check the ball free to Pinoe, who launches a beautiful fifty-yard ball to Alex Morgan. Alex makes a run straight toward the Japanese goal, her speed springing her free before she slots a leaning left-footer into the far corner, her second goal in two games. It's a pretty good way to start a World Cup career for Alex, who is twenty-two and our youngest player.

Japan has had its best World Cup ever, and they've done it four months after an earthquake and tsunami devastated the country's northeast coast and killed more than fifteen thousand people. Thousands more were left homeless. One of the country's professional teams had to cancel its season. All through the tournament, the Japanese coach and players said they hoped they might bring comfort and inspiration to their devastated homeland.

No, we do not think they are going to go away.

With less than ten minutes to play, Japan takes advantage of a turnover in our end and a misplayed clearance and ties the score. The battle heads into two fifteen-minute extra time periods.

Pinoe and Alex team up again, and Alex launches a cross that Abby buries with a vintage header. We go up 2–1, with less than five minutes left. Again Japan answers, this time with Homare Sawa, their captain, who is playing in her fifth World Cup. She redirects a corner kick with a deft flick of her foot.

So it comes down to PKs again. Paul Rogers goes over the lineup, and Boxxy steps to the spot first. Ayumi Kaihori, the

Japanese keeper, dives left and stops the ball with her foot. The Japanese shooter, Aya Miyama, who scored Japan's first goal, converts, and now it's my turn. I stride up to the 18, pick up the ball, and walk purposefully toward the spot, bouncing the ball twice as I go. I place it down and step back. I make my approach. I want to go to the upper left, the same direction as I went against Brazil, but with a little more power. I strike the ball well, but I am leaning back a bit and get under it.

I am sick almost the moment the ball leaves my foot. The ball skies over the crossbar. I can't believe it. I overhit it. I was so positive I would bury it. I rub my left hand over my face, turn away from the goal, and walk back to my teammates, never a fun walk to make. People say a few things to pick me up. They mean well, but it doesn't help much. Japan goes up 2–0, and now Tobin Heath is up. Tobin, who had come on for Pinoe, goes lower left, but Kaihori launches herself to the right and parries it away. We have taken three PKs and missed them all. Abby finally drills one in on her turn, and now it's on Japanese midfielder Saki Kumagai. If she makes it, Japan wins and we lose. If she misses, we have life.

Kumagai places the ball down and has to wait for Hope, who is trying to freeze her a bit, standing in her bright yellow uniform a few steps off the line. The referee tells her to get in the goal. Hope stretches her arms horizontally, as if she were a basketball player boxing somebody out, then raises her arms overhead and jumps up and down, trying to occupy every possible inch of space in the goal, trying to look as big and imposing as possible.

Saki Kumagai rips the ball into the upper left corner. Hope has no chance. The whole Japanese team runs out on the field. The emptiness I feel could fill oceans. If we have to lose, I'm glad it is to Japan, a country that has been through such a horrible ordeal, but that perspective mostly comes later. Now I can't get much beyond thinking I came up very small for my country. I know it is not just me. I know others missed and that we win as a team and lose as a team. I just expect way more than this from myself.

"Don't worry," James says. "This is not going to define you. You are just going to keep getting better and better."

It is a hard night, a long night. I can't sleep. I keep replaying the PK. Maybe more than anything in my whole soccer career, I want that PK back. But there are no mulligans in soccer.

12

WONDER IN WEMBLEY

EVEN IN DEFEAT, the U.S. Women's National Team is bigger than ever. Abby's epic goal against Brazil seems to have transfixed the whole country. The final game against Japan draws 13.5 million viewers, a soccer record for ESPN. Somebody tells me there were seven thousand tweets per second during the final. There were plenty of doubters after we lost to Sweden, but America loves a good comeback story, and we are that.

Hundreds of fans are waiting at our Frankfurt hotel to welcome us, treating us as if we'd won the PK shootout. I do spots on *The Daily Show, Good Morning America,* and CNN. Abby, Hope, and Alex are the breakout stars, but all of us are much more well-known than we were even a week earlier.

It's all good, but James has me convinced that I have much more improvement left in me, and that is where I turn my attention. For years I have been doing a lot of fitness work on my own, beyond the national team workouts, because I knew I needed to. Now I am doing even more. At tournaments, I sneak out of hotels to get in a distance run. Or I knock out a set of 800-meter runs, supplementing them with push-ups and sit-ups and ab work. I want to be at my strongest when others are starting to falter. I want to be the American Steven Gerrard, setting up teammates, creating chances, orchestrating the attack with quick feet and inexhaustible energy.

The goal for 2012 is to peak at the London Olympics, and everything seems on course. We finish the Algarve Cup with a 4–0 thrashing of Sweden and then head to Japan for two friendlies, one against Japan and the other against Brazil. The day before the game against Japan, we tour the city of Sendai in the northeastern part of the country, one of the areas ravaged by the earthquake and tsunami almost exactly one year before. I look from the bus window at a vast expanse of debris and shells of houses and battered boats. The destruction goes on for miles. It is one of the most chilling spectacles I have ever seen. I can't even imagine what it must've been like to live through it. Soccer seems totally inconsequential when you think about the scope of the devastation and the deaths.

|||||

About six weeks before the Olympics, we play a friendly against China before a packed house at PPL Park in Chester, Pennsylvania. It's just across the Delaware River from my home, so I've got a bunch of family and friends there, though not my parents. Four years since I was kicked out, I am still an ex-Lloyd in my parents' world. We're wearing our new red-striped "Where's Waldo" jerseys on a day so hot the pitch feels like a griddle. It's the Sunday of Memorial Day weekend.

Nothing memorable comes out of it for me.

Nothing memorable at all.

Not including a meaningless post–World Cup Victory Tour friendly in the fall of 2011, I have started forty-one straight games for the U.S. Women's National Team since returning from my broken ankle almost two years earlier. I get a rousing ovation when I am introduced to a hometown crowd before the game, and then I play forty-five forgettable minutes before Pia subs me out for Lauren Cheney.

Most of our team struggles through an uninspiring half; it's hard to believe we are the same side that played such strong, cohesive soccer in the World Cup final against Japan. We blast long balls up the field like rec players. Our back line gets panicky in the face of high Chinese pressure, and it spreads. We turn the ball over, make sloppy passes, leave openings for China to attack. Somehow we wind up with a 2–1 lead at the half, and I still can't tell you how.

Whether it's because I am trying too hard in front of my people, I don't know, but I am out of my element from the outset, losing the ball, playing helter-skelter, failing to convert two excellent chances inside the box. When Pia makes the switch, I am distraught. I am embarrassed. I go out with family and friends afterward, but I have a hard time enjoying myself. I am in replay mode, maybe not as much as after I missed the PK against Japan, but close.

Jill Ellis, an assistant coach under Pia, knows me as well as any coach in the national program and knows my predilection for beating myself up. She texts me and tells me to keep my head up, reminding me it's one game and not to give it too much weight.

Dawn Scott, our fitness coach, also texts me. "Keep fighting and move on," she says.

I head home for an eight-day break. I don't hear from James for three full days, which is very unusual. He tells me later that he wanted me to sweat it out for a bit and think about my mistakes. I spend the time training hard and thinking harder. I am doing an upper-body workout in my garage when I finally hear from him. I'm still beating myself up, and it's in that moment that I realize that I can't have anyone at my events anymore. It changes things. I put too much pressure on myself to please people. I know I shouldn't, but I do. Brian is planning on coming to London for the Olympics.

"Please don't," I tell him. "I hope you understand it's not about you. It's about me."

My mind continues to race:

I can't believe that it's still possible for me to have a game like this, after all the work I've put in. I thought I was beyond this point. I hate it. I hate that it's staying with me. Hate that it's affecting my confidence.

We leave for a trip to Sweden and two games against the Swedes and the Japanese. In our first training session, I don't feel well. I do okay, but mentally I might as well be in Greenland. I don't even want the ball. I haven't felt like this in a long time.

Jill keeps trying to lift me up. One day Pia calls me up to her room to talk.

"What do you think went on in the China game?" she asks.

"I don't know; I was just off that day, and it was weird because I had been doing really well in training. I'm human. It was just one of those days, I guess."

"Well, I just want you to know I believe in you one hundred percent," Pia says. "If there is anything I can do to help you when your game is a bit off, please let me know."

"I will. Thanks," I say.

We have a couple days off of training, and I run both days. Before the first game, Pia wants to talk again. She comes in my room and tells me that I am not starting.

"Cheney has been doing well, and she deserves to start," Pia says. "But it's going to be you and Boxxy and Cheney in the midfield during the Olympics, and we're going to need all three of you. Just stay ready and make the most of your chance when it comes."

Though I can't say I am shocked by this news, it is still tough to hear. I know I had a poor first half against China. I still think Pia is overreacting. I've been a fixture on this team for a couple of years. I've come up big in important moments. To get yanked from the lineup because of one bad half seems extreme.

I do not tell Pia that. I sit on the bench, smoldering. When Pia calls for me to replace Boxxy, I do everything I'm supposed to do. I sit back and defend and tackle hard, play some good balls, and create chances. We win 3–1, and then we play Japan and I don't start again. Pia comes up to me in the locker room beforehand and is smiling and laughing and puts her arm on my shoulder.

"How are you?" she asks.

"I'm great," I say.

"Watch Cheney and Boxxy. You are going to come in at halftime."

I am still angry and play with an edge when I come on in the second half. I work hard on both sides of the ball. We win 4–1, and I can't wait to get on the plane and get back home so I can work with James and train my butt off. I want to prove to Pia she should never have taken me out of the starting lineup. Sometimes I have to work hard to find a slight to motivate me. I don't have to work hard at all this time.

I am going to show Pia Sundhage.

We head out to Sandy, Utah, for our last friendly before we head to London for the Olympics. Pia must be enjoying these meetings with me, because she calls for another one.

"What do you think of your last two games?" she says.

"I think I did what I needed to do when I came on," I say.

"What do you think you need to do to get back in the starting lineup?" she asks.

"The same things I have been doing," I say.

"How would you compare yourself to Lauren Cheney as a player?" she says.

This strikes me as a very odd question, an inappropriate question. I don't know what she wants to hear from me. I just tell her the truth.

"First of all, Cheney and I are completely different players with different strengths. Second of all, I don't like to worry about other people or compare myself to them. I worry about myself and what I can bring to the team."

Pia nods approvingly and again seems as if she wants to build me up.

"You were the best player we had in qualifying. I hope you know that," she says.

I thank her, and before I leave, I want to tell her one more thing — that the bad half against China was not going to define me, any more than the missed PK was going to define me.

"It hurt my confidence and I held on to it for a long time — too long — but I am fine now, and I am ready to fight back," I tell her. "I won't let you or the team down. I will fight and keep fighting, and I will win this battle."

Pia's jaw drops, in an almost cartoonish way. I don't know why. Maybe she's impressed that I said all the right things. Who knows? She tells me again that she is going to need all three of us in midfield, and that sometimes I may play with Boxxy, other times with Lauren. Sometimes I will be attacking, and other times I may have to sit back and mostly defend.

"I'm ready to do whatever needs to be done," I say.

I return home from Utah for one last blast of training with James and go at it as hard as ever. I land on Saturday and am on the field playing against a Universal Soccer Academy boys' team a day later. All week, I do what James calls "physical power" training, with sets of sprints from 100 meters up to 800 meters, along with hill work, upper-body circuits, and distance runs every day. Heather Mitts, my teammate and fellow Universal Soccer student, is doing some fine-tuning with James and thinks I am overdoing it in a big way.

"You aren't going to be able to get through the Olympics if you keep up this pace," Heather tells me. "You will never last. You are going to burn out. I really think you need to back off."

I know Heather means well, and I know I must look like a maniac, pushing so hard before the biggest tournament of the year. But I also know this is exactly what I need—for my mind as well as my body.

I don't let up once I get to England. I have to secretly go out and do my workouts. Our first full day there is an off day for the team. I go for a ten-mile run and then on another day do three three-minute runs at 70 percent effort, 80 percent, and then 90 percent—nine runs in total, all on a treadmill. I also do doggie sprints behind a building near our hotel after one of our training sessions. We have a team outing to a medieval castle. It's cool, but I am too wrapped up in the present to think about the Middle Ages. When we get back,

Pia comes into my room and officially lets me know what I already know . . . that I will not be starting in our first game, against France.

"This is not about you doing anything wrong. You've been playing well. We're going to need you, so stay ready," she says.

"I'm ready," I say.

James tells me, "If you want to be ready — truly ready — then you need to start visualizing. Start the process a few days before the game. Be quiet and centered with mental images of playing this game against France. See yourself on the field. See the game unfolding in your mind. Trust me, it will make a big difference."

So I start visualizing more intently than I ever have in my life. I sit in my room, shut my eyes, listen to music, and visualize. I go on walks and visualize. I visualize that our team is down against France and I come on to score the winning goal.

All the extra work, mental and physical, has done just what I hoped it would. I feel strong and fit and confident again. We have a scrimmage against Norway and we win 2–0, and I am on top of my game, getting lots done.

"You were awesome today, Carli," Heather tells me.

"Thanks. I feel good," I say.

We travel up to Glasgow, Scotland, for our opener against

France. It starts about as badly as it can. We fall behind 2–0 in the opening fourteen minutes, and then Boxxy goes down a couple of minutes later. She's been battling a calf injury for the last few weeks now, and you could see in training that she was not 100 percent. Boxxy tries to gut it out, but seeing the grimace on her face, I know there is no way she can continue.

Pia summons me off the bench, and after the briefest of warm-ups, I am in our Olympic midfield sooner than I ever imagined.

Abby scores on a header off of a Pinoe corner, Alex pops a bouncing ball over the French keeper's head, and we're even before the half is over.

Playing holding mid, I am careful not to do too much or get caught upfield too far. I am keeping my touches to a minimum, focusing on strong tackling and clean passes. Ten minutes into the second half, Pinoe tracks down a loose ball that the French have given away, near the right sideline. I am pushing upfield. There's some space in front of me, and Pinoe sees it and delivers a perfect square ball to my feet. I settle in with my right foot and follow with a quick one-two that ends with a flick with the outside of my right foot. In an instant, I am clear of a closing defender. I have just enough room, about twenty-five yards out on the right, and I let it rip. Baseball sluggers talk about how great it feels when they hit a ball in their sweet spot. This ball is in my sweet spot. It rises like a tracer and rockets into the upper left corner of the net. We're up 3–2. I run toward the U.S. bench and get hugs from Pinoe and everybody.

Alex scores another goal off a scramble in front, and we've answered another challenge in a big way.

I guess this visualization stuff works, I think.

After a typically exciting tournament night—ice bath, stretch, hydrate—I go for a light twenty-minute run the next day to loosen up and get ready for our second game, against Colombia. They're a rapidly improving team with several extremely dangerous players.

Colombia comes at us with feet flying. It's a chippy game, but you can't get lured into payback or playing with reckless anger. The best revenge is always to win. In the thirty-third minute, Pinoe strikes a high, bending ball from distance after Alex picks a Colombian pocket. Abby makes it 2–0 with a sliding, angled right-footer with under twenty to play. I have spent the whole game doing my midfield housekeeping, winning balls and distributing the ball quickly. Just a few minutes after Abby's goal, I play a ball ahead to Lauren Cheney, who finds Pinoe to her right. I see a channel up the middle in front of me, and off I go, a full sprint into space. Pinoe tucks a perfect ball on the floor to me, in stride, and after a touch in the box, I slide it under the onrushing keeper into the left side of the goal.

Two games ago, I was a veteran who had lost her starting spot and whose Olympic role was murkier than the English Channel. Now we have two victories behind us and I have two goals behind me.

Chester, Pennsylvania?

I don't even remember playing a game there.

We win a hard-fought battle with North Korea on a goal by Abby and move into the quarterfinals against New Zealand. It's another scrappy game, and I am a bit off at the outset, but I play my way into the game and keep up my high work rate from box to box. Abby finishes a pass from Alex to give us a 1–0 lead in the twenty-seventh minute. Then, with about twenty minutes left to play, I settle a bouncing ball and take a touch as I start upfield. I see an opening up the middle, where Alex is making a run. I chip a forty-yard ball, and Alex gets in behind the defense and is alone on the Kiwi keeper, Jenny Bindon, who rushes off her line and goes into a slide as Alex sprints at her full blast. Alex tries to leap over her, but her left knee slams into Bindon's face, and the two of them go sprawling as the ball trickles away. The keeper takes the worst of it by far, but Alex has to come off. Pia replaces her with Sydney Leroux. We don't want to lose Alex, for sure, but Syd steps right in and buries her first Olympic goal to seal a 2–0 victory.

It's not our prettiest game, but we keep advancing, and Hope and the defense deliver our third straight shutout. We move into the semifinals with Canada in Old Trafford, home of Manchester United and one of the most storied soccer stadiums in the world. The Canadians know us well, and they are playing at a high level under their new coach, John Herdman. Nobody forgets the scrap they gave us in our overtime victory in the quarterfinals at the Beijing Games, and they have the ever-dangerous Christine Sinclair.

Three different times in Old Trafford, Sinclair gives Canada a one-goal lead. Three times, we answer. The game seems to get more intense by the minute. It is not always a showcase for the Olympic ideals. In the fifty-fifth minute, I am on the ground in the box, and suddenly there is a foot stomping on my head, driving it into the pitch.

It's as dirty a play as you will ever see. A stud on the bottom of the boot slams into my temple, maybe an inch from my eye. The culprit is Canadian veteran Melissa Tancredi, who commits seven fouls in the game, including one in the first minute. Tancredi's foot stomp — which should've been a red card — somehow goes unnoticed.

I get up and keep going. That's what our team does too. Pinoe scores our first two goals, the first one on a curling corner kick that sneaks inside the near post, and the second on a wicked, angled strike from distance. We're still down a goal in the seventy-eighth minute when Erin McLeod, the Canadian goalkeeper, goes up to grab a corner kick and falls to the ground to secure it. McLeod, like virtually all keepers, often takes longer than the six seconds the rules allow a keeper to get rid of the ball. Abby is counting loudly — "One, two, three, four . . ." — to make sure that the referee, Christina Pedersen of Norway, is aware of McLeod's tardiness. McLeod dribbles the ball a few times and lets go with a dropkick, and Pedersen blows her whistle.

Nobody knows what is going on, until it becomes apparent Pedersen has called McLeod for delay of game, giving us an indirect kick. I have never seen this call made in a game, let alone a game of this magnitude. I am not worrying about it, though. I got my head stomped, and there was no call.

The ref owes us one.

Tobin Heath touches the ball on the kick, and Pinoe rips a blast toward the goal. As Canadian defender Marie-Eve Nault turns away to shield her face from the shot, it caroms off her arm. Pedersen blows her whistle again, this time for a PK.

The Canadians are enraged. Abby is calm, stepping to the spot and knocking a low shot inside the left post to tie the game, her fifth goal in five Olympic games.

Abby very nearly wins it for us about six minutes later, when Alex makes a cross from the left flank, toward the right of the goal. Abby is crashing the net hard and gets the ball on her foot. I am sure the ball is going in the net, but Abby's sliding shot veers just wide of the near post, and into overtime the semifinal goes.

All I can think of as we prepare for two fifteen-minute overtimes is that this is what I train for, to be able to keep pushing on, finding gears I don't know I have. In games like this, where the outcome can swing on the smallest of events — a tackle at midfield, a high-pressure run that forces a sloppy pass, a sprint to keep a ball inbounds — the last thing I ever want is to feel I didn't leave it all out there. It's a cliché, I know: give it your all, never say die . . . all of that.

But you know what?

This is exactly what winning championships takes . . . keeping the foot on the pedal, even when you are on your last drop of gas. So I dig deep. We all dig deep. I can't tell you for sure that we want this game more than the Canadians, because their players have shown great heart the whole game, but I can tell you this: We are going to do whatever it takes to win. We won't stomp on any Canadian heads, but we will battle to the end.

Near the end of the first overtime, Canada's Diana Matheson makes a good run down the right side and crosses to Sinclair, who is gunning for number four when Rachel Buehler breaks it up just in time, forcing a corner kick. Now it's the end of the next overtime, and after good chances for both teams, Alex gets space and arches a cross to Abby. Abby goes up. I feel as though I've seen this movie a thousand times in my career. I know the ending by heart:

Abby goes higher than anybody else, using all of her height and power and skill.

Abby's forehead meets the airborne ball.

Abby snaps her head forward.

The ball rips into the goal.

All of that happens, except the last part; Abby's header bounds off the crossbar. The game stays tied. We move into the third minute of extra time, 123 minutes into the match, when Heather O'Reilly, who came on for Lauren Cheney in the 101st minute, gets off a cross from the right side. There is a crowd in front. I see Alex measure it and go up, a pink headband rising above the fray, connecting with the ball, knocking a looping header right over McLeod's hand, into the net.

It is our first lead of the whole game, and a very good time to get it. Seconds later, Pedersen looks at her watch and signals the game's end.

The Canadians are understandably bitter, especially Sinclair, who was so brilliant throughout.

"We feel like we didn't lose; we feel like it was taken from us," Sinclair tells the media later. "It's a shame in a game like that that was so important, the ref decided the result before it started."

I'm not buying the conspiracy theory, and not giving it a moment's thought. We have more important things ahead of us—such as a return engagement with Japan. In the 2007 World Cup, we lost to Brazil and then got another shot at them in Beijing in the Olympic gold medal game.

In 2011, we lost to Japan in the World Cup, and now we get another shot at them in the final in London. I like the symmetry.

|||||

Wembley Stadium is one of those holy places in sports, a building you walk into and feel the history pouring out of every one of the ninety thousand red seats. The current Wembley dates only to 2007, but it's on the same patch of North London land as its predecessor. It's still home to the English national team and still the site of the biggest football game of the year in England, the Football Association (FA) Challenge Cup championship. So to me, Wembley is Wembley.

I am thrilled and honored to be here.

After a day of rest following the Canada marathon, we have a light training session and go over final preparations for Japan. It's our fourth meeting of the year against them, so we don't expect any major surprises. We know how good the Japanese are on the ball and how they like to attack defenses in precise, quick-footed waves, and they are masters of the one-touch pass. We have to stay organized.

The biggest adjustment for me in this final is that I am back to my regular position as an attacking midfielder. Boxxy's injury has healed, and she has returned to the lineup at holding mid, so that frees me up to attack more. I am all for that.

Maybe it's the historic setting, or the gold medal that is on the line, or the expectations I have now that I am back at attacking mid, but I am a bundle of nerves for this Olympic final. I have hardly been nervous at all in the previous games. Now it's as if every nerve ending in my body is plugged in.

We board the team bus from the Olympic Village, and I head to my usual seat, a couple of rows from the back on the right. Hope is in the seat across from me, the way she always is. When you look at team photos, especially candid ones, Hope and I always seem to be next to each other, and it's no accident; the bond we forged through the World Cup ordeal five years before only gets stronger. More than anybody else on the team, she is there for me, and I know she always will be. That counts for everything in my world.

We arrive at Wembley about ninety minutes before kick-off. James, of course, has sent me his usual get-your-mind-right email, which I've read so often that I practically have it memorized. The message isn't just empowering; it is real. It centers me and calms me. I reread the email on the bus. It's almost a meditative exercise by now, like listening to a harp or the sound of the sea. It's so easy before big games for your mind to race and get so cluttered that you go out and try to do way too much, which does nothing but work against you. I distill the essence of his message in my own self-talk:

Let the game come to you.

Keep it simple.

You have been training for years for this moment. Nobody has worked harder to be here. Now let your training take over.

All you have to do is be Carli. Have fun. Play as if you are on Ark Road or Vermes Field. Play with the same passion you had as a little girl on Black Baron Drive in Delran, New Jersey.

Play the game you love.

I walk off the bus, headphones in place, listening to Chris Brown's "Dreamer" as I go. It lifts me up. We file into the locker room. It's spacious and bright and has a pink LONDON 2012 logo on the floor. It is bigtime. I have a corner locker, next to Heather O'Reilly, my longtime Jersey pal and team-mate.

Minutes before we are to walk out onto the pitch, the coaches leave the room. Pia has gone over strategic stuff the night before, reminding us to apply high pressure, tackle hard, win fifty-fifty balls, be strong in the air, and use our size to our advantage. We know that such a technically superb team as Japan will almost certainly control possession in the game.

"Don't worry about that," Pia said. "Let's just stay orga-nized defensively, and we will be fine."

Pia isn't one to give rah-rah speeches, or any other sort of speech. She leaves us on our own, and we all huddle up. Christie Rampone, our captain, talks, and then Abby talks and a few others chime in. I don't say anything. All I want to do is get on the pitch and play.

We file out of the locker room, high-five the staff as we head down the hallway, and get lined up for the pregame walk-out. I am hand in hand with a little blond girl. When we step onto the pitch, I cannot believe the size of the crowd. More than 80,000 people, the largest crowd ever to see a women's soccer game, are in those red seats. It is a staggering sight, a beautiful sight. They are here to see us, to see women play soccer. I am a jumble of energy and anticipation. We shake hands with the Japanese players and listen to the two national anthems. Finally, it is time to play.

When the whistle blows, I feel like a bull that has just been let loose on the streets of Pamplona.

I am so ready.

We kick off, and Abby rolls the ball to Alex, who plays it back to me. Pia likes us to play long ball at the start, maybe to help us get our legs pumping and blood going, so I send it long upfield toward Abby. Barely a minute in, I intercept a pass for Japan's great midfielder, Homare Sawa, and off we go on the counterattack. I don't make much of a cross at the end of it, but starting the game with a strong defensive play always stokes me up even more.

In the eighth minute, Japan makes an uncharacteristic mistake and loses an easy ball out of bounds. Pinoe throws in to Boxxy, who passes the ball across the field to Kelley O'Hara. Kelley knocks it on to Tobin, who makes a run down the left flank and makes a nice pass inside the box to Alex. Alex gets instant separation, sprints to the end line, and makes a great cross.

I see this unfolding near the 18 and make a hard run toward the goal, leaving my mark behind. Abby is in front, ready to finish. I see Alex's ball floating toward me and keep running hard toward the goal. The cross is sinking fast. Abby, to my right, has her left leg raised, ready to side-volley it in, though a defender is right on her. I have a clear lane in front of me and see the ball coming at me, as big as a beach ball. I lower my head, hit the ball squarely, and drive it into the net.

Most people think Abby scored until they see the replay, but Abby and I actually joked that I stole her goal. I go running and sliding in celebration, arms outstretched, and soon my teammates are on top of me. It is a dream beginning. We are on the board and ready for more.

The Japanese have started tentatively, but they are firing up fast. In the seventeenth minute, Christie Rampone saves a goal after a defensive breakdown with a brilliant block with her right foot, and Hope follows by stuffing the rebound. It's a close call. Hope is even better when, just over a minute later, Japan's Yuki Ogimi puts a head on a cross and launches it toward our goal. The game is an instant away from being tied, but Hope dives and punches the ball into the crossbar. Ogimi tries to pound in the rebound but misses wide. Hope has saved us again.

Japan keeps the pressure on, its attack now humming. Aya Miyama, the Japanese captain, pounds a ball into the crossbar in the thirty-fourth minute, and we dodge another bullet.

None of us ever thought this would be easy.

Ten minutes into the second half, Pinoe plays a square ball to me not far from midfield. I take a touch and see a stretch of space in front of me, with only one defender to beat. So I take off with the ball, veering to the right. I take two more touches, and then a few more, and I still have room. Still going right, I notice the defense, and the goalkeeper, are all going with me, and at that moment I know it is time.

I am about twenty-five yards out. I take a final touch and let it rip, across my body, across the grain. I hit it squarely. I watch the ball's flight, watch it all the way until it flies into the side netting, just inside the left post.

Wembley explodes in noise. I run around, looking for people to hug.

We are up 2–0.

There are thirty-five minutes to play, an eternity and a half. Nobody believes this is done. Nobody. Japan came back twice in the World Cup, and there is no way they are quitting now. The Japanese are pushing the attack, committing numbers. Ogimi converts a rebound with a side-footed shot that Hope has no chance on in the sixty-fourth minute, and it is 2–1. Japan keeps coming. We try to stay tight and organized. In the eighty-second minute, Lauren Cheney pushes a left-footed pass to me, and I have space and let it fly, a left-footed laser that feels good when it leaves my foot but sails inches over the crossbar.

Darn.

That could've clinched it.

It's a one-goal game, and the most skillful team in the world is coming at us. In the eighty-third minute, Mana Iwabuchi, a nineteen-year-old forward, pressures Christie as she is receiving a pass, steals it, and goes in alone on Hope. Iwabuchi takes a left-footed touch, then a right, and then side-foots a shot toward the far post, from maybe ten yards away. It looks to be a certain goal, a tic game. Hope sees Iwabuchi, sees the ball on the side of her right foot, reads it perfectly. Hope dives to her left. She knocks it toward the corner.

It is a world-class save. She has had several of them in this game.

Hope has to smother a dangerous cross in the next minute, and you just know it's going to be frantic right until the final whistle. The game goes into stoppage time, and now it's the ninety-second minute and Japan is making its last push. A forward named Karina Maruyama gets the ball on the right and starts to attack. I make a hard run at her, contesting her advance, getting in her way enough so that she trips me. The referee blows the whistle for a foul. Hope takes the ensuing free kick and sends it far downfield. The ball never returns to our end. The three whistles sound. The crowd roars.

We are Olympic champions, again.

We hug and cry and revel, and I look up at this massive, holy place we are in — Wembley — and disbelief only begins to describe it. We have just defended our Olympic gold medal.

In Wembley Stadium.

Could it get better than this?

The medal ceremony is one of the greatest moments of my life. I listen to "The Star-Spangled Banner," and even though we won in 2008, somehow this is so much richer, so much better. I love our team and love how we fought, and on a personal note, I feel so much satisfaction knowing that I started the Olympic Games as a reserve and finished them in a whole different place.

This isn't about me, though. It's about a group of women who fought hard and gave every morsel of energy and skill they had to offer. It's about sacrifice and belief and never giving in, or giving up. It's about character — one of the Five Pillars James talked to me about from the start.

13

COACHING CAROUSEL

I ARRIVE HOME FROM THE OLYMPICS still in a full state of euphoria, with my second gold medal around my neck and my first and only boyfriend, Brian Hollins, waiting for me at Newark Liberty Airport. My aunt Patti and uncle Wayne, cousins Jaime and Adam, and Jaime's husband and their two kids are all there. So are my aunt Sandy and Brian's mother and sister and her husband and their two kids, along with my best friends, twin sisters Kathy and Karen Sweet, and friend Laura Aleszczyk. (James isn't there, but that's only because he prefers to sit out the celebrations and let me revel with my family and friends.) They've arranged for a party bus to take us all back down the Turnpike to my place in Mount Laurel, which they've decorated with an American flag, posters, and USA placards. There are red-white-and-blue hearts, and a homemade sign that reads: WE ARE SO PROUD OF YOU, CARLI.

Everyone is wearing either a number 10 jersey or an Olympic shirt or a T-shirt with a silhouette of me kicking a ball.

It's a small and heartfelt celebration, just the way I like it.

My parents and brother and sister are not are part of the festivities, by their own choice. I don't hear from any of them after the Olympics, though they do send me a card. I can't believe it has been four years since we've had any relationship to speak of.

It's all so crazy and needless, and so sad, but after all this time, I am getting resigned to it. I would be thrilled if all this went away tomorrow and we could be whole again. I will meet them wherever I have to meet them. I will own my part in it.

James has encouraged me over and over again to find a solution. He does it again when I get back from London.

"You need to reach out to your parents. You both made mistakes, and you need to find a way to try to reunite with your family," he says. "Reach out to them and be open. You can fix this. Sit down and have an honest conversation and put it behind you."

The problem again is that our family doesn't do these conversations well. Somebody flies into a rage, someone else reacts, and soon accusations are flying like buzzards over roadkill.

A few weeks after my return, my brother reaches out and wants to come over. It's awkward at first. We make small talk. Then we get to bigger issues.

"I just want you to know how much this hurts Mom and Dad every single day of their lives," Stephen says. "They want you back in the worst way. I just hope you can see how unfair you've been with them."

Then my brother tells me, "You don't give yourself enough credit. You were destined to be this sort of player, an Olympic champion."

This is family code for "James doesn't deserve all the credit you give him."

Stephen stays for a couple of hours. I don't see much change going on, but he asks if I would consider getting together with Mom and Dad.

"I'm going to think about it," I say.

I decide to invite my parents over to my house. I've been in it for more than four years, and they've never really even seen it.

My parents come over a couple of weeks after my brother's visit. We start with chitchat, but we all know we're not here to talk about how lovely an autumn it has been.

"I am sorry that I've been disrespectful at times," I say.

"I was wrong to be that way after all that you've done for me."

"I am sorry I snapped that day when I told you to move out," my father says. We are off to a pretty good start. I allow myself to be hopeful. If we can at least respect each other's feelings, maybe we can get somewhere. If both sides can own their hurtful behavior, we have a chance.

I give my parents a tour of my home. "It's so nice," my mom says. "We're so proud of what you're doing and that you can live in such a beautiful home." They sit on my couch and we start to talk, and I own up to everything they have had an issue with. I find out, finally, about my dad's heart surgery and how he had a 90 percent blockage and had to be rushed to the hospital. All in all, it's as good a visit as we've had in a long time. My dad has to get up early for work, so they leave after a few hours.

"We'll reach out and get together again soon," my mother says.

"That sounds good," I say, and then I hug each of them and say goodbye.

When they leave, I have a feeling I haven't had for a long time in regard to my family. I have hope.

IIIII

Things may be taking a turn toward stability with the family, but not so on the team. Pia Sundhage is out as coach. It is announced on September 1, 2012, in Rochester, New York, Abby's hometown, hours before we are set to begin our victory tour against Costa Rica. It is twenty-three days after Pia led us to our second Olympic gold medal. Pia, true to form, uses the moment to break into song before the crowd, this time Dylan's "If Not for You."

With a five-year record of 89-6-10, Pia is returning home to coach the national team of her native Sweden and says she is "so happy." She praises all of us and thanks us and her assistants for making her look good.

"Before I took this job, I always admired the spirit and character of the U.S. team, but to experience that firsthand on the training field and from the bench as their coach was truly special and something I will treasure for the rest of my life," Pia says.

U.S. Soccer president Sunil Gulati is no less gushing about Pia and says it was an awfully difficult decision to let her go. Everybody wants to make it sound as if Pia is the one who engineered the change, but I'm not so sure.

Pia and I have had our differences here and there — I was furious when I was benched before the Olympics — but I have always had great respect for her as a coach. She is positive and clever and humble, and she made us a much better and more creative team. People forget that she took over a team in complete chaos after the 2007 World Cup, that she gradually brought Hope back into the fold and stabilized things. Two Olympic golds and a runner-up finish on PKs in the World Cup final is a pretty good body of work in five years.

I am going to miss Pia Sundhage.

IIIII

Our new coach—number three during my time with the team—takes over on January 1, 2013. He is a fifty-eight-year-old Scotsman named Tom Sermanni. He coached Australia to three World Cup quarterfinal finishes and helped make the Australians a much more skillful and technically proficient team. Tom also coached in our defunct pro league, the WUSA, and is known for a laid-back temperament and for being a players' coach, a man who lets players play and treats people like grownups.

Tom has strong credentials and seems to be a very nice man. If you are going to make a coaching change, this is the time to do it—with no truly major tournaments coming up until the 2015 World Cup in Canada.

We begin 2013 with a training camp in Jacksonville, Florida, in early February. Tom is trying to get a feel for all of us as players and experimenting with different combinations, a smart thing to do. He isn't saying much at the start, mostly watching. I take nothing for granted. I approach every training session as if I am fighting for a spot on the team, going for my first cap. I don't want anything to determine my fate other than my play.

A friend says to me, "Relax, Carli. Do you think you really have to prove yourself at this point?"

Relaxing on the field isn't in my DNA, especially when there's a new coach on board.

"I don't know what Tom thinks, or what he's been told," I reply. "I'm leaving nothing to chance. I'm going to empty the tank every day."

We head to Portugal for our annual Algarve Cup appearance. We open against Iceland. About fifteen minutes in, I am shoved from behind and land hard on my left shoulder. I hear a crack. Cracks are rarely good. This time is no exception. I get right up and keep playing, but I know something is wrong. My arm feels weak and painful. I can't push off with it at all and have to keep it right at my side when I run. I finish the half and get it looked at by a doctor and trainer.

The doctor doesn't think it is serious and says my strength in it is actually quite good.

"You should be able to play with it," he says.

I am heartened by the diagnosis, but I have my doubts. The crack I heard wasn't from stepping on an acorn. I start the second half and go for almost twenty minutes until the pain gets to be too much. Tom subs me out and brings in Christen Press.

We beat Iceland, 3–0, but it's hard for me to enjoy it. The pain is much worse the next day, after the adrenaline wears off. I ice it and get treatment and am so ticked off this happened, it's making me crazy. I go for a run on a treadmill because I don't want to lose fitness. I do sprints at practice with my left arm dangling like a loose thread, but there's no getting around the facts: I am going to be a spectator for the rest of the Algarve Cup.

The pain persists, keeping me up at night, so I lie in bed and have a movie marathon until dawn. I am hurt, and I am worried. I have been rehabbing and doing everything necessary to feel better, get my strength back, and get back on the field, but it's not working.

I was planning to play in the final, but the doctor wants me to get an MRI and X-ray to make sure nothing serious happened. We get the results immediately. The images show a break in the greater tuberosity, the top part of the humerus bone in my shoulder. I am told I cannot play.

We play Germany in the final and win 2–0, but I am out for the game and the next six to eight weeks.

I miss a team trip to Germany and the Netherlands as I let my shoulder heal. The shoulder responds well to the rest and the rehab, and the eight-week X-ray looks good, so I am cleared to play. I head off to Buffalo to join the Western New York Flash, my new team in yet another incarnation of women's pro soccer. This one is called the National Women's Soccer League. I hope it gets some traction and outlasts its predecessors, the WUSA and the WPS. Abby, the local kid made good, is the star of the Flash, and it's great to be together.

We win the first two games before Abby and I head off to a weeklong national team camp. We play solidly in a 3–0 victory over Canada, but then it's back to Buffalo, where I score my first goal in front of the home crowd. It's wacky bouncing back and forth between the Flash and the national team, but we know that the league needs the national team players if it's going to have a chance at survival.

You do what you have to do.

||||

The national team's next friendly is in Jersey at Red Bull Arena, against South Korea. We're undefeated in ten games under Tom, and though there is some grumbling about his ever-changing lineups, you can't argue with the results. In the tenth minute, Abby gets nice service in the box from Lauren Cheney, settles the ball with her left foot, pivots, and drills a ball in the near side for a 1–0 lead. Eight minutes later, I carry the ball in midfield and flick a pass out wide to the left. Cheney is on the ball again, lofting a cross in front, where Abby delivers — yes — a diving header to make it 2–0. The goal ties Abby with Mia Hamm atop the all-time U.S. scoring list with 158 goals. The tie does not last for long, because before the game is a half-hour old, Abby knocks in another header off a Pinoe corner kick, and now she is alone at number 159, the greatest soccer scorer in American history.

I rush toward Abby to hug her, and so does the whole team. Our bench players sprint out onto the field in their green pinnies. The crowd stands and cheers. It is a beautiful moment. Abby and I haven't always been on the same side of things, but I've always admired her love of the game and the indomitable strength and will she brings to the striker position. She loves to score goals and she loves to win, and to her everlasting credit, she loves to share the glory. She credits her teammates for making her look good. Abby has always been that way, and it says a whole lot about her as a person. I am happy for Abby that she breaks the record, and happy again when she scores number 4—number 160 overall—in stoppage time of the first half.

If four goals in a half and setting a cherished record were not enough, Abby also accepts the captain's armband from Christie Rampone after Christie is subbed out. When it is Abby's time to come off, she hands it to me. It may seem like a minor matter in the middle of a blowout victory, but it isn't to Hope Solo. Our star goalkeeper is not on the roster as she recovers from surgery. But later she sends me a text: "It is awesome to see you get the respect you finally deserve. You will always be my captain."

It is one of the most touching messages I've ever gotten.

|||||

During another trip back to Jersey with the Western New York Flash to face Sky Blue, I want to keep the positive momentum going with my parents. They tell me they are planning on coming to the game.

"Great. I will leave you tickets," I say. I haven't seen them in four months because of my commitments with the national team and the Flash. My cousins and aunts and uncles and other friends are coming to the game as well. I am just hoping everybody can get along.

"It'll be good to see you," I tell my parents.

My parents bring along my aunt Lorraine, my father's sister. We have a strong game, and I score a goal and am looking forward to visiting with everyone afterward, especially my parents. They haven't been to one of my games in a long time. They were there when I was with the Delran Dynamite. My father was the one who always set up his folding chair by the corner flag, to get the best possible view of my attacking game.

When I get to the meeting area, I don't see my parents anywhere. I am puzzled. I hope everything is okay. I ask Brian and my cousin Jaime if they've seen my parents.

"No, I think they left," Jaime says.

"They left? Why would they leave?" I say. I think, *There's no way they would just leave without saying anything to me.*

But I am wrong. They didn't wait. For whatever reason, they left without even saying hello.

As Brian and I drive away from the field, my mom sends me a text message: "Hi, Carli. It was great to see you play in person. Sorry we didn't see you after the game. We knew you had a lot of people there and didn't want to keep you from seeing them. Love, Mom and Dad."

I haven't seen my parents since.

IIIII

The Flash gets better and better as the season goes on. In a game against Washington, Abby sends the ball to me all game, and it is my turn to fill the net. I score three times in a 4–0 victory. I earn NWSL Player of the Week honors, and we go six weeks without losing a game, securing a playoff spot against Sky Blue, a team we've beaten twice.

We beat them 2–1 in the semis, but then wind up losing the final to Portland, which gets a sick goal from Tobin Heath from about thirty-six yards out. It's not the ending I am looking for, but it's been a good year on the whole, and I return to the national team in strong form. We finish the year undefeated, with a 4–1 victory over Brazil. I have a part in three of the four goals. We seem to be flourishing as we head into 2014 and World Cup qualifying, a team that seems ready to reach a new level and cement its status as the best women's soccer team in the world.

It's too bad it doesn't work out that way.

14

COACHING CAROUSEL PART II

I FEEL STRONGER AND FITTER than I ever have in our first camp of 2014 in Los Angeles. My shooting is off in training and that is annoying, and I am thinking a bit too much on the field, but otherwise I am ready to crush it this year.

The mood teamwide is not as good.

We don't start well in a friendly against Canada. I am sitting the game out after getting two yellow cards in our last game against Brazil. We have some new pieces in new places, and the result isn't up to our usual standard. The first twenty minutes are okay, and we do wind up winning on a goal by Sydney Leroux, but our possession and creativity are lacking.

It is not what Tom Sermanni is looking for from the top-ranked team in the world.

We beat up on Russia in two games in February—combined score 15–0—and head off to Portugal for Algarve, a tournament we've long dominated. We've won three of the last four titles and eight of the last eleven. But we are a team in flux. Abby hasn't been at the top of her game, so Tom meets with her and tells her she is behind Press and Leroux in the lineup right now.

We open against Japan, and Abby is sitting. We have a number of opportunities early but don't convert. I score on a left-footer from the right side early on, but it is called offsides and does not count. We finally break through in the fifty-ninth minute, when Syd runs at the Japanese keeper, gets a piece of the ensuing goal kick, and watches it trickle into the Japanese goal. It is as bad a gaffe as you will ever see a keeper make, but Syd's hustle makes it happen. Aya Miyama ties it in the final seven minutes on a thirty-five-yard free kick that Hope doesn't get a good read on.

Two days later we take on Sweden, coached by our old friend Pia. It is so strange seeing her on the other sideline.

Abby is starting because Syd came down with something, but the day doesn't begin well. About fifteen minutes in, Amy Rodriguez gets hauled down in the box and Abby steps up to the spot, but the Swedish keeper makes a diving stop of her PK. Sweden takes the lead not even ten minutes later on a beautiful, lunging header by veteran Lotta Schelin.

We dominate the flow of play and have numerous chances but can't convert anything, including a couple of breakaways that Hedvig Lindahl stuffs us on. The 1–0 loss is our first in forty-three games. It means we have no shot at winning the tournament this year. It also means the grumbling about Tom will start to get louder.

Tom is a master strategist with a great feel for the game and very much a laissez-faire approach to things. He isn't big on structure or planning. I like him and his effort to make us a more sophisticated and creative team, but right now our results on the field are not what we are accustomed to.

Next up is Denmark. We fall behind 3–0 in the first half, the first time in the thirty-year history of the U.S. Women's National Team that has ever happened. We wind up closing to 4–3 in the sixty-eighth minute, after I make a cross of a short run in traffic on the left and Pinoe finishes it off a deflection. Press and Pinoe narrowly miss tying it up. We lose 5–3 and finish with our worst Algarve result ever — seventh place.

Tom is disgusted, and so are we. He says our touches were sloppy and our giveaways contributed greatly to the result in this tournament.

After an eighteen-day break when most of us return to our NWSL teams, we reconvene for a twelve-day camp in Denver. There is a weird vibe almost from the time camp begins. On the first day, we work on crossing and marking in the box and play small-sided games; we have done none of these things under Tom. Jill Ellis, now the program's technical director, is here to observe and record training sessions. I hear that Dan Flynn and Sunil Gulati are supposed to be coming into camp, another curious development if it's true.

All I know is that the World Cup qualifying starts in six months and we need to start getting better every single day, beginning now. We don't want the excitement we put ourselves through in 2011, when we had to beat Italy to qualify. If we have any shot at winning the World Cup for the first time since 1999, the work and commitment needs to start here.

Our next game is against China in Commerce City, Colorado, on the first Sunday in April. We play with a new alignment—4-3-3 as opposed to 4-4-2—and are much better. We're passing well, making runs off the ball, generating all kinds of threats, finally breaking through when the former Lauren Cheney—now Lauren Holiday—slams in a ball from the top of the box late in the first half. Pinoe curls in a direct kick through heavy traffic in the second half, and we come away with a one-sided 2–0 triumph.

We are in the bus going back to the hotel when a team staffer gets up.

"Sunil and Dan want to meet with the team at seven thirty tonight," the guy says.

We gather in the hotel and soon Sunil and Dan arrive,

along with the coaching staff, but not Tom. So now we know why everything has felt so odd.

Tom Sermanni is out of a job, fired not long after losing the only two games he ever lost as head coach of the national team.

Sunil tells us this is not just a knee-jerk reaction to what happened in Portugal. He has nothing but admiration for Tom as a person and as a coach. Sunil says it basically comes down to a "subjective evaluation of where the team is going."

"It just wasn't working. We think we need to go in a different direction, stylistically, or whatever you want to call it," Sunil says. He says that Jill Ellis will take over on an interim basis.

Several players start to cry after the announcement is made. I feel sick about it. I know we haven't played at our usual level, but I did not see this coming at all. When Sunil and Dan leave, Tom comes in and speaks to us.

"This unfortunately is part of sport," he says. "I'm thankful for the opportunity to coach you, and thank you all for your effort and hard work. It's been an honor to coach you, and I wish you all the best going forward."

When Sunil, Dan, and Tom are gone, we discuss everything among ourselves. Lauren, Abby, and Christie all talk while I take it in, until I have something to say.

"One thing that I think will really help us as a team is to

stop complaining when there are issues or we're not happy with something. If an issue needs to be addressed, approach that person. We need to be more up front with each other. We need to stop all the chatter, because it's destructive and it's contagious."

Later, I visit Tom in his room.

"How are you holding up?" I ask.

"I'm okay, Carli," he says. "Thank you. You are playing at a very high level, and I hope you keep that up. You are a true professional, and all I can say is, I wish I had twenty players with your attitude."

"I appreciate that, Tom. You've done nothing but give me support. You're handling this in a classy way. You're a very good coach, and I know you will land on your feet."

I sleep horribly that night. I keep thinking about Tom and all this sudden upheaval so close to World Cup qualifying. Whoever is coaching us, we need to get it together.

We fly to San Diego for our next game, also against China. The night before the game, we all hang out in Jill's room and have s'mores, team-bonding over chocolate, graham crackers, and marshmallows. It's light and fun.

I am totally fired up for this game. I want to start this new era off right, to send a message. We come out flying. I have a great chance in front in the opening ten minutes, but I knock it just wide. We keep pushing. Ten minutes later, I one-time a carom off of Holiday and rip it past the keeper to get us going. Three minutes later, I get some space twenty-five yards out and let fly with a lefty dipper that rockets inside the left post. It's my fiftieth career goal, and I find out later it puts me ninth on the all-time U.S. scoring list. Syd finishes the scoring with an angled left-footer on the ground. I get Player of the Game, and it makes a good day even better.

So the Jill Ellis Era is off to a 1–0 start, and it continues in Winnipeg, Canada, in May — the same city where we will open our World Cup in thirteen months. Jill, officially, is still the interim coach, but I am positive she will get the job. She is well respected and has been around the program a long time. She knows the team as well as anyone. Jill has a series of positional meetings in our Winnipeg hotel and asks to meet with me before our friendly against Canada. We meet in Jill's hotel room.

"It's time you stepped up and took a leadership role on this team," she says. "You have earned your stripes. You've won gold medals. You've scored in the biggest games. You have earned the respect of everyone with the way you work and your commitment to the team, and now it's time for you to put the team on your shoulders and win the World Cup. No matter who is coaching this team, you need to do this."

I sit and take in what Jill is saying. I don't say anything at first. It's the biggest vote of confidence I have ever gotten from a coach. I've liked Jill from the first time I met her when she coached the U-21 team. She is someone who sees the positives in a situation and then works at fixing the things that aren't positive.

I thank her for her faith and agree that it's time for me to be more out front in how I lead.

"I am ready to do whatever it takes—*whatever it takes*—to bring the World Cup back to the United States," I tell her.

Supported by a big and enthusiastic home crowd, the Canadians take a 1–0 lead. We are not at our best, but we are fighting hard. Abby gets robbed by Canadian keeper Erin McLeod, a little payback for the whole one-two-three counting gambit in the 2012 Olympics. I run a give-and-go with Abby that leads to a cross in front to Heather O'Reilly, but her shot caroms just wide. Syd scores a late goal with a timely finish off a defensive misplay, and we get away with a 1–1 tie.

A week later, U.S. Soccer makes it official: Jill Ellis is the eighth head coach of the U.S. Women's National Team. I am thrilled for her and thrilled for our team, because I know that Jill is the perfect fit for us. She's smart, knowledgeable, and experienced, and though she is friendly and approachable, she is nobody's pushover.

I text her as soon as I hear: "Congrats on the job! Real happy you got it, now let's go start the road to winning the World Cup."

Jill replies: "Heck, yeah. So dang excited. I cannot wait to see you in Tampa. ☺"

Tampa comes around in a couple of weeks, Jill's first camp as head coach. There's an infusion of energy and enthusiasm, and though we don't play our best game, we defeat a strong French team, 1–0, and then have a return engagement in East Hartford, Connecticut, five days later. Jill names me captain for the game and tells me again that she wants me to be a leader and be more vocal. Tony Gustavsson, a Swede who Jill just named as her top assistant, meets with me before the game. He shows me clips from the first France game and says the team needs me to push higher up on the field and impact the game more by using my attacking skills.

"You can win games for this team, and we need to get you into a position to do that," Tony says.

"I want to attack. I love to attack," I tell him. "And I totally agree that I can help the team even more by pushing higher."

We play France to a 2–2 tie, and I feel much more active and impactful in the middle of the field. I have worked my butt off for years for every coach I've ever had, but I can't deny that I feel a special connection with Jill. We have very different backgrounds — she grew up in England and didn't start playing soccer until her family moved to Virginia when she was a teenager — but in so many ways, we are the same. I am, at my core, an introvert, and so is Jill. I just want to be with my people, and so does Jill. Neither of us wants to be fussed over. We're both transparent, and all that does is make me want to play even harder for her. Jill Ellis is one of the most authentic people I've ever met. I love that about her. I think she is going to do great things with this team.

‖‖‖

The whole year has been pointing toward World Cup qualifying, and it is finally here, with an opening game against Trinidad and Tobago in Kansas City. I am in the attacking third a lot. We are creating all sorts of chances but don't break through until the fifty-fifth minute, when I play a through ball to Alex Morgan, who cuts left and crosses to Abby, who heads it in. That lone goal holds up, and we move on to Chicago, where we take apart Guatemala, 5–0. Next we move on to Washington, D.C., for a CONCACAF semifinal against Haiti. Jill and Tony talk beforehand about scoring early in this game to assert our dominance. I oblige, chesting a punchout from the Haitian keeper to the ground, then half-volleying a shot into the corner to make it 1–0. Abby scores twice, and the onslaught is on. The final score is 6–0, setting us up with a date against Mexico in Chester, Pennsylvania. The winner will advance to the World Cup.

It is my first game back in this stadium since the game against China before the 2012 Olympics when I lost my starting spot. It is also a prime chance to pay back Mexico for beating us in qualifying four years earlier. These things may not seem like a big deal, but when you play so many games, over so many years, these extra layers of motivation are important. I want to crush it in Chester. I want to crush Mexico. I want to expunge every bit of the unsavory memories I have of both, so it is straight from my script when Tobin Heath lofts a beautiful cross early on. I am in front, unmarked, and head it into the goal. I follow with a PK goal after Tobin is dragged down in the box. We win 3–0.

We are going to the World Cup in Canada.

I wish we could start playing today.

15

CHARACTER BUILDERS

JILL ELLIS HAS A PLAN, and nobody much likes it. She schedules a long, four-game trip to Brasilia, Brazil, one apiece against China and Argentina and two against Brazil, right before the end of the year. Jill has her reasons.

She feels we need some adversity, to face some hard challenges. And this trip will have a lot of them. The fields are bad. Everything is more complicated. We're in our off-season, and she's bringing us halfway across the world to be booed by eighteen thousand people. All of this is to make us uncomfortable, to prepare us to face whatever challenges lie ahead and be able to adjust.

We open against China, and we are not sharp at all. As a team, we are coming off of a six-week break and our fitness level isn't very high. Plus, we're not possessing the ball well. I flick in a low, hard cross from Pinoe to make it 1–0 midway through the first half, but the rest of the game is marked mostly by missed chances and low-energy play. I am not happy with my game or our collective effort. China scores in the second half for a 1–1 finish. We need to do much better against Brazil a couple of days from now.

Things start auspiciously when I score on a spinning left-footer in front in the sixth minute. When Pinoe follows with a drive from the right into the side of the net, we are up 2–0, not even twenty-five minutes in. We have many other opportunities to add to the lead, but we don't capitalize. At the other end, we are giving Brazil way too much space. We are not applying high pressure, instead letting Brazil come samba-dancing out of its own end. Marta scores on a beautiful through ball, then scores again on a deft, angled left-footer. In the sixty-fifth minute, she breaks the 2–2 tie by beating Hope on the near side with a shot from distance. It's a ball Hope saves forty-nine times out of fifty, but this one gets past her. Now we have to play catch-up.

We do not catch up. We aren't playing quickly enough, and our defensive shape is lacking. The crowd roars when the match ends and we trudge off, without a victory in two games.

After an off day, we demolish Argentina, 7–0, behind four goals from Press and three from me. But the real test

Long-range strikes are one of my favorite parts of the game. Here I tee one up against Japan in London.

One of my all-time-favorite celebration photos. It was a happy pile of players when we took the lead against Japan in the Olympic final in London.

Arm in arm with my best friend on the team, Hope Solo, minutes after we beat Japan for the Olympic gold in 2012.

Showing our gold Olympic medals when we won in London.

A full-service midfielder has to do it all. Here I go up for a header against Colombia in the knockout round of the 2015 World Cup.

Not too many people thought we'd beat Germany in the World Cup semifinals. My PK got us on the board—and on our way to a 2–0 victory.

I was pumped after my first goal in the 2015 World Cup final! Check out the bulging veins.

The Cup final was three minutes old when my first goal came to rest.

The celebration was on after I scored number 2 against Japan in Vancouver in the World Cup final.

When the great Abby Wambach came on late in the World Cup final, it was only right that I took off the captain's armband and presented it to her.

Jill Ellis gets a major bear hug after the World Cup final.

I was happy to win the Silver Boot as the second leading scorer in the 2015 World Cup, but nothing came close to winning the Cup itself.

There's nothing better than being on top of the podium and bringing the World Cup trophy back home after sixteen years.

The stuff of dreams: holding up the Golden Ball after being named the best player in the 2015 World Cup.

A happy reunion of family and friends greeted me at the Newark airport on my return from the 2012 London Olympics. That's my former teammate Heather Mitts to my immediate right.

The ultimate World Cup celebration: a ticker-tape parade in New York City with Megan Rapinoe and, of course, the trophy!

My husband, Brian Hollins, and I have prime seats at the 2015 ESPYs in Los Angeles.

President Barack Obama graciously invited the World Cup champions to the White House. He seems quite pleased with his new jersey.

The USWNT coach Jill Ellis and I were honored by FIFA as World Coach and World Player of the Year at a Swiss gala in January 2016. Playing for Jill has been one of the best things that has ever happened to me.

TODAY EXCLUSIVE

U.S. WOMEN SOCCER STARS FIGHT BACK
FILE EQUAL PAY COMPLAINT OVER WAGE GAP ISSUE

TODAY

N HOLDS A CAMPAIGN RALLY TODAY AT SUNY PURCHASE   FORMER PRESID 7:33 | 52°

In the spring of 2016, my U.S. teammates (from left) Alex Morgan, Hope Solo, and Becky Sauerbrunn, and I (along with Megan Rapinoe, not pictured) filed a federal wage-discrimination complaint. That's our attorney, Jeffrey Kessler, on the right.

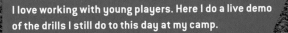

I love working with young players. Here I do a live demo of the drills I still do to this day at my camp.

will come when we face Brazil in the final, four days before Christmas.

The coaches make it clear we are not going to give the Brazilians the space they had in the first game. We respond by not giving them any space at all. We have already heard Marta's name far too often over the PA system. We pretty much park the proverbial bus and sit back in our end, and the Brazilians can't break through. We open it up a bit in the second half. Becky Sauerbrunn knocks a beautiful header that the Brazilian keeper punches into the crossbar. I score on a left-foot shot in front off a cross that is nullified by an offsides call. The game finishes in a scoreless tie, and though we are better and more organized, we're not close to where we need to be.

If Jill wants us to be uncomfortable, the trip to Brasilia can only be seen as a major success.

At this point, all I want is to be home, to be with Brian, and to get back to training with James. I need to reconnect and recharge. Two days later I am back in Jersey, I am in the Blue Barn, doing repeat sprints and working on shooting. On Christmas Eve, I run seventy-five minutes and do some upper-body work and already feel way better than I did in Brazil. It feels good to push myself hard. I can't let up. There's a World Cup in six months. The prep work starts now, even on Christmas Day.

Christmas is my favorite holiday. It has been since I was a little girl. Our family would always go get the tree together; sometimes we'd even chop one down. We'd decorate it with lights and ornaments, including my favorite — a little globe with a baby inside it. I don't know why I liked that one so much. Maybe the innocence, the purity of it. Christmas felt magical every single year.

On the night before Christmas, we'd all be together as a family — cousins and aunts and uncles, usually at Aunt Patti's house — and then we'd go back to our house and open our presents on Christmas morning. My parents would separate the gifts into piles, one each for Carli, Stephen, and Ashley. It felt different from every other day of the year. I loved that it was cold out and that everybody was happy. That was the best part. This is the seventh Christmas I've spent apart from my family. It's always a little sad for me to think about that. One day I hope we can celebrate Christmas together again.

I spend Christmas Day 2014 at Brian's sister Lisa's house, but before I go, I head out to Laurel Acres to run the hill for my workout. Nobody else is in the park, and it's cold. It's a great, energizing workout. I always train on Christmas Day.

For me, it's an affirmation of how committed I am, how I am ready to go even on the most special holiday of the year.

I train right through the New Year. Our camp starts on January 5, and when departure day nears, it's never a fun time. Brian and I have gotten very good at saying goodbye because we have had way too much practice, but the closer we get, the more difficult the goodbyes get.

"You know, one of these days we will actually be together and not have to do this all the time," I tell him.

Three days before I am to head out to Los Angeles, Brian suggests we have a belated anniversary celebration of the day we started going together, December 20, 2000. He wants to drive to a charming little enclave in Bucks County, Pennsylvania, called Peddler's Village. The cluster of antique stone buildings and nice shops are done up beautifully with lights and decorations for the holidays. We're going to stroll through the cobblestone streets and do some exploring and then have a quiet dinner at a place called the Yardley Inn.

It's a Friday night, and as we walk through Peddler's Village, Brian is unusually quiet. He seems preoccupied. I hope nothing is wrong. I don't know what's going on, but I decide to let it go.

"You want to have a cup of hot chocolate?" he asks.

"Sure," I reply.

We stop at a café, and Brian looks around for an empty table. There are none—and that seems to annoy him. We stroll with our hot chocolate, and then Brian suggests we walk over to a gazebo. It's normally very private there, but at the moment it's full of gingerbread houses and people looking at the gingerbread houses.

We keep walking. I am on Brian's right, before he suddenly circles around to the other side of me. Now I am on his left.

Brian is definitely not himself, I think.

Through the quaint streets of Peddler's Village we go, until we come upon a tunnel decorated with little white Christmas lights twinkling all around us. Brian stops in the tunnel.

"Let's take a picture," he says, holding out his phone at arm's length.

Brian never wants to take selfies. I wish I knew what was up with him.

And then, a moment or two after he puts his phone away, Brian Hollins falls to one knee, right in the middle of the tunnel. He reaches for my hand.

"I've been waiting to do this for a very long time," he says. "Carli, you are the love of my life, and I want to spend the rest of my life with you. Will you marry me?"

I start to tear up before I can even say yes. Brian waits for a herd of people in the tunnel to go by and then reaches into his inside coat pocket and hands me a small box. I open it up. It is the most beautiful engagement ring I have ever seen. I slip it on, and it fits perfectly.

It is the happiest moment of my life.

||||

Jill believes that if we are going to be the best, we have to play the best. There's no sense in going into the World Cup with a series of 5–0 victories behind us that make everybody feel good but are as useful as a flat tire when it comes to our preparation. So after a hard four-week camp in Los Angeles in January, she wants to test us in a big way.

"One of the first things I did when I got hired was to tell people, 'We haven't won the World Cup in sixteen years,'" Jill says. "'If we want to change that, we can't continue what we've been doing.' That's not a knock on the previous coaches. Not at all. It's just we need to find ways to create challenges and build a stronger team. I told them I wanted to play the top five teams in the world if we can — boom, boom, boom, boom, boom. We've never played a series of games against the best. Maybe we've played one or two, but that is not enough. I want us to go into the World Cup hungry and humbled, and understanding that to win, it's going to require us paying close attention to all the details."

So the start of our World Cup year begins with games against France and England before we head to Portugal for the Algarve Cup. The only top team Jill couldn't get scheduled is Germany, just because the available dates were not a match.

Jill is determined to keep stretching our comfort zone as if it were Spandex, and she is no less determined to tighten us up and organize us defensively. Pia and Tom both were more inclined to give us room to solve problems on our own. Jill wants to lay down a more disciplined, structured defensive foundation—a system in which we are defending as a unit and staying organized and building out from there.

It is a sound plan, and it needs to be, because we are playing without Hope. She has been suspended by U.S. Soccer. The start in goal goes to Ashlyn Harris, not an easy spot to be in while starting a World Cup year against the number-three team in the world.

The game against France is every bit the test Jill wants it to be. We have multiple chances to score. I have a great one inside the box, but I sky it over the crossbar. Abby gets stuffed on a penalty kick. We never break through, and the French score twice. The 2–0 defeat is the first time we have ever lost to them.

The most disconcerting thing for me, personally, is where I am on the field. Jill starts me at left mid, telling me that she wants me to pinch in toward the middle. She's thinking that being in the wide position may help me get forward faster, which is what she wants. I understand her thinking, and I understand she wants to give Lauren Holiday and Morgan Brian a look in the middle of our 4-4-2 alignment. But the truth is, I don't think it works on the field.

Holiday is in the middle for the first sixty minutes. Then Jill moves me there, and I see immediate payoffs. I feel much more involved in the attack; I am winning balls and starting counters. The middle is where I want to be. I believe it is where I need to be, for the good of the team.

Jill sticks with the original alignment, with me out wide at left mid, in our next game against England, and though we score a 1–0 victory on a goal by Alex Morgan, I am frustrated by the way I play—and where I play. I miss a great chance to score on a volley, all the more maddening because I'd taken about two hundred of them with James the week before. I talk to James, and I agree with his assessment that I am not mentally preparing myself to play—not spending enough time visualizing the game and how I want to play.

"You will always play better when you've already visualized

the game in your head," says James, who also tells me not to get worked up about the position issue.

"Embrace the change that Jill is making. Be a good soldier. Learn something from it. You are seeing the field from a different perspective. It will make you a stronger player when you are back in the middle."

For now, though, I am still on the left, pinched in, and fixed on erasing the memory of the Algarve debacle of a year earlier — the seventh-place finish that basically cost Tom Sermanni his job. It's important that we make a statement this time around, start putting pieces together.

We open up the Algarve Cup against Norway and fall behind by a goal on a header right before halftime. We apply more pressure in the second half. Ten minutes in, I spin on a ball just outside the box and drive a left-footed shot inside the far post to tie the game. I convert a PK off a hand ball in the box six minutes later, and we make the lead hold up.

We move on to beat Switzerland, 3–0, in a bruising and mostly artless game.

Assured of a place in the final, Jill rests several starters, me included, for the first half, in a scoreless tie with Iceland. We are playing too cautiously, and I honestly think it goes back to the losses to Brazil in December and France in February. We have taken on a distinctly defensive posture and are mostly looking to score on counterattacks. I want to take it to the other team. I want to come at them and see if they can stop us.

We have a rematch against France in the Algarve final. Hope is back from her suspension, so that's a huge lift. Julie Johnston scores on a well-aimed header on Holiday's perfectly placed direct kick, and Christen Press slices through the spine of the French defense to give us a two-goal lead. Hope stops a PK and is awesome, and we come off with a 2–0 victory.

Even though Jill is ecstatic with the win, I have a different take. It was a strong defensive game, no doubt, but we continue to sit back and play passively, as if we're afraid that if we push forward, we're going to leave ourselves vulnerable. We sustain almost no attack against France and have few good chances. I feel largely uninvolved and barely even touch the ball. Of course I am happy with the result, but the manner in which we achieve it is troubling, not because everything must revolve around me, but because we're honestly not playing at a high level. Sometimes scores can fool you, mask an underlying issue. When I get back to my room, I write in my journal:

We have a long way to go to win the World Cup.

After a twelve-day break, we return to camp in L.A., and one day we scrimmage against a boys' team. Again, I am not happy with how we play. I am out wide on the left, and

Lauren Holiday and Morgan Brian are in the middle. I feel almost useless, like a fifth wheel. Jill walks up to me after the scrimmage. For maybe the first time in my life, I break down on the field. Even I am shocked at the depth of my emotions in that moment.

"What's wrong, Carli?" Jill asks.

I can barely get any words out, I am so frustrated. Jill looks at me and says, "Let's meet later." I nod and wipe the tears away and get it together. Later that night, Jill texts me.

"What are you doing?" she says.

"I'm in my PJs, getting ready for bed," I reply.

"I'm in my PJs too. Why don't you come up to my room for a few minutes and we'll talk?"

When I get to Jill's room, her daughter, Lily, is asleep in the other bed. I start talking about this left-mid experiment and how I think it is not working for anybody. I am not alone in this opinion, either. Abby, for one, is telling me constantly that the team needs me in the middle of the field. Others are saying the same thing. I'm not looking to be insubordinate, but rather to openly voice an opinion about the direction of the team.

"I respect you totally and will do whatever it takes and whatever you want, but that's how I feel," I tell Jill. And then, suddenly, I break down again, emotions sweeping over me in tidal waves, my voice shaky and cracking.

"I'm so frustrated. I just want to help us win," I say.

"It's okay, Carli. It's okay," Jill says. She listens to everything I have to say and tells me that she's glad I am being honest with my emotions. She has a kind and comforting way about her.

"I know you want what's best for the team. You have always been team-oriented, from the first time I coached you," Jill says. "Listen, we just wanted to try some things. It's a process we have to go through, and sometimes there are struggles when people are in different roles. I've watched these games and spoken with the other coaches, and everybody seems to agree that we need you back in the middle. You did very well outside, but it's not the same when we don't have you in the middle of the field.

"We're going to be better for having gone through this, and so will you, I think. But don't you worry. You will be back in the eight."

Eight is the number soccer coaches use to refer to a traditional center midfielder. Eight is where I want to be. It is a great pajama talk. I go back to my room feeling much better about things.

We travel to St. Louis to play New Zealand on April 4, one day before the Cardinals open their season in Busch Stadium. More than 35,000 people turn out, the biggest crowd for a standalone friendly we've ever had. I feel short on confidence as the game begins, weighted by pressure to prove to Jill I was right. The best antidote to that is to play simply, get into the flow of things, help with the buildup.

That is exactly what I do.

I am taking a few touches, moving the ball around, getting people linked up. Just five minutes in, I play a ball back and it swings wide to the left, where Meghan Klingenberg is overlapping. I see space in front of me and make a run into the box, and Kling finds me perfectly. I carry the ball in and flick a centering pass as Amy Rodriguez and Christen Press crash the goal. The ball is deflected away, but it is a strong offensive thrust by us. I am heartened, no matter that we didn't score. This is how I want us to play.

Kling hits a blistering shot from outside the box to open the scoring, and we add three more late goals in a six-minute span for a 4–0 victory. It is the best game we've played in a while, and the most gratifying game I've played in a while too.

The World Cup is two months out, and it's crucial to keep building toward a peak. We have three more friendlies left.

It's time to do all the fine-tuning we can, to work on all the details that Jill says could well make the difference in Canada.

More than that, it is time to regain our defiance and swagger, our drive to do whatever it takes to win a ball, make a stop, make the difference.

We take care of Ireland, 3–0, on Mother's Day. Abby scores two goals, which is a great sign. Abby doesn't get the minutes she used to, but she is still a finishing dynamo, a proven difference-maker. Having her confident and in a good place going into the World Cup is huge.

Abby buries two more goals in a 5–1 rout of Mexico a week later. Sydney Leroux scores twice as well, her best game of the year. From start to finish, we are firing at Mexico from near and far. I feel super-fit and confident, and I return home for one last break before the World Cup. I run the hill at Laurel Acres and do intervals on the track, grinding out rep after rep with James watching. I feel explosive, and I want to be even more so. I want to be able to take two steps toward a loose ball and leave everybody in my rearview mirror. This isn't training for the sake of training; it's training with a purpose.

It's training to win a World Cup.

"You are going to have something left in the tank when everybody else's is empty," James tells me.

Our sendoff game before the World Cup is right at home, in Red Bull Arena in Harrison, New Jersey, against South Korea. Brian is there, and so are Jaime and my other friends. My parents and siblings are not there. There has been no contact. It's not something I can focus on right now. I want to crush it in this game. I want the perfect farewell before we head to Winnipeg, Canada, for the biggest soccer tournament of my life.

Our performance as a team in a 0–0 draw is well short of our best. The media pretty much buries us for not pounding South Korea. While our approach is more direct, and less effective, than it has been, I am trying not to be worried about it.

Who gets all worked up about the last game of spring training?

No, it is not a vintage U.S. game, but negativity is like quicksand: you hang around it enough and it will take you all the way down. You will never be heard from again. I am hard enough on myself that I can make my own negativity, so I really don't need any help.

I am named the Player of the Match against South Korea, and though we didn't get a victory, I'll take it. I am fitter than I have ever been. I have been training for this for years and feel more ready for this tournament than any I have ever played in in my life.

In June 2015, we take a charter flight to Winnipeg, Canada. My third World Cup is days away. Neither of the first two went anything close to the way I had hoped.

It is time to change the narrative.

16

DISAPPEARING ACT

I AM LOOKING AT MYSELF on a computer screen, and the images aren't pretty. I am in our team meeting room in our Winnipeg hotel, sitting at a long folding table, flanked by Jill Ellis on one side and her assistants, Tony Gustavsson and Steve Swanson, on the other. It is the day before we open our World Cup against Australia, and Jill and Steve want to show me video clips of various fouls I've committed in some of our recent games. Most were for coming in from behind or for putting a little too much crunch into my tackles. One of them came in the first half against Mexico just a few weeks earlier, when I went in late and hard on a sliding tackle.

I got whistled for a foul but didn't get a card, even though I could have.

The point of the video review is to caution me about excessive aggression. Of course they want me to be physical and make clean, hard tackles, but they also want to remind me that two yellows in the World Cup group stage means you sit for a game.

"We just need you to be careful," Jill says. "We don't want you to change your game. We want you to make good tackles and win possession for us. Just don't go overboard with it—maybe throttle it back a bit, especially when you are coming in from behind."

I get it.

"Believe me, the last thing I want is to miss a World Cup game," I assure them. "I'll be careful."

I file a mental note about it and go for a walk in downtown Winnipeg. I sit by the edge of a fountain. The sound of the flowing water is soothing. I start to write in my journal. I have been keeping a journal since I first made the national team in 2006. Besides being therapeutic, it gives me an in-the-moment record of my thoughts and feelings, successes and stresses, a competitive and emotional archive. The day's entry focuses on the great place I am in mentally, the supreme self-belief that comes when you feel that you are truly a better player than you have ever been.

I have never been more ready to play. I am relieved to know that Brian, Jaime, my aunt Patti, and everybody else knows not to come to Canada. I debate whether it seems harsh not to share this experience with them, but I know how I am.

If they were here, I'd be thinking about them and wanting to be sure they're okay. I had family at my two previous World Cups, and we know how those went.

I do not want to go for the hat trick.

I am rooming with Hope, and she always has the TV on to check out games in other groups from all over Canada. I don't want to watch one second. I just want to play. That's it. I am completely in a mental bunker.

IIIII

Day breaks sunny and warm on June 8, 2015. I sleep well and have eggs, yogurt, and fruit — my usual pregame meal. Once breakfast settles, I head out for my fifteen-minute game-day run, down St. Mary Avenue in downtown Winnipeg, past streets named Hargrave and Donald and Smith, toward the Red River. When my watch hits seven and a half minutes, I turn around and start back. I stretch and hydrate and shower, then have a light lunch — salad and fruit. I never eat anything heavy on game days. I want to feel light, hungry.

Outside our hotel we pass through a gauntlet of fans who cheer as we board the bus for the short ride to the University of Manitoba. I head for my seat in the back, cue up "Dreamer" on my iPod, and reread the email James sent.

In the locker room, Jill gathers us together and goes over

some last-second strategic reminders. After she's done, I sit quietly and await the walkout. I am feeling oddly out of sorts. My legs are leaden.

You'll feel better when you get out there and start running, I tell myself.

The stadium is packed, and it's so loud and overwhelmingly pro-America that we might as well be back in the States.

Australia kicks off and applies pressure almost immediately. In the fifth minute, Australian Emily van Egmond blasts a shot that Hope stops with a diving punchout. Moments later, I touch the ball for only the second time in the game and give it away deep in our end. No harm comes of it, but I am sick that I did that.

You are better than that. This is the World Cup you've been waiting for years for. C'mon, Carli. Raise your game, I tell myself.

The game continues. We are playing poorly, losing possession, knocking random long balls up the field. I don't complete my first pass until the ninth minute. I make a strong tackle for a takeaway and hope that it is something to build on and get me into the game.

It is not.

I don't feel like myself. I feel passive. The leaden sensation never lifts. I can't stop thinking of the film session with Jill and her assistants, and I can feel myself backing off too much, almost becoming a bystander. Going in hard on tackles isn't just a trademark of mine; it's a part of my game plan. I always make a point to have a crunching tackle early in a game. Not to be dirty or to cheap-shot anybody. Just to let my opponents know what they are going to be up against when they are pressing the attack in the midfield. It's another item from the James playbook: crunching tackles early can set the tone for an entire game.

But against Australia, I am not crunching. I am barely even tapping. It's all so weird. I am just not myself, and we as a team are not ourselves either. Pinoe scores on a deflected strike, and that's about the only good thing I can say about the first half—even though we've been outplayed throughout, we are tied at one. We have our savior in red—Hope Solo —to thank for that. After the early stop on van Egmond, she turned away two more dangerous chances that easily could've left us looking at a two-goal deficit at the half.

Jill has made it clear throughout the run-up to the World Cup that we don't want to peak too early. It is, after all, a monthlong tournament.

"I am not looking for us to play our best game against Australia," she said.

She need not have worried.

We are playing defensively, allowing Australia to dominate possession. Lauren Holiday and I, the center-mids, are under instruction to play as number sixes — or holding midfielders — and play the ball out wide. We're not connecting with the forward line, threading through balls, or changing fields. It feels as if we're stuck in neutral for almost all of the ninety minutes. Australia is a solid and improving side, but the Aussies have never beaten us, and you never would've guessed that watching the first half.

I feel horrible in the locker room at halftime, low in energy and spirits.

The second half starts better when I make a good strip in the opening two minutes, but then I have too much weight on my pass and it rolls out of bounds. On and on it goes for me. I make a promising run after delivering a pass, but it misses the mark and goes the other way. We raise our game enough to take a 3–1 victory on second-half goals by Press and another one from Pinoe, but we can't fool ourselves by the final score. It was a sloppy effort almost from start to finish, and Hope bailed us out.

My number-one objective going into our second group game — against Pia Sundhage and Sweden — is to wipe my mental hard-drive and reboot. There is nothing else to do. I resolve to start now, to join the battle in our second game and bring all I've got.

Unfortunately, I do anything but that on the field.

I spend most of the ninety minutes trying to be perfect, instead of just playing. I am not attacking, not taking risks, and playing with a strange reticence, like a swimmer who dips her toe in the pool but is afraid to dive in. Most of our team seems similarly afflicted, and with Sweden staying compact and organized in its end, our chances are few.

The highlight for me is when I play a good ball forward to Press. She plays it off to Pinoe, who threads it back to me as I make a run on the left side. My leaning, left-footed strike is batted over the crossbar by the Swedish keeper Hedvig Lindahl, and the game remains scoreless.

It's a quality save, but not nearly as good as Meghan Klingenberg's. Standing on the goal line during a scramble off a corner kick, Kling watches Sweden's Caroline Seger artfully flick a ball with the outside of her right foot toward our goal. Hope is out of the play, and it seems to be a lock to go in, before five-feet-two-inch Kling jumps as high as she can go, heading the ball into the crossbar and safely away. The game ends 0–0. We are atop Group D, but you would never know it by the way we are getting ripped for our listless, unimaginative play, especially on the offensive end. Our back line and

Hope have been superb. That is what we have morphed into, a defense-first side that doesn't want to commit numbers on the attack and is displaying a lack of patience and skill when we do attack.

After the game, when Jill asks Holiday and me to meet with her, the topic is all about our defensive angles and how we can't let ourselves get split when we're defending.

I walk out of that meeting feeling even worse.

I am not even defending the right way, I think.

We fly west to Vancouver for our third Group D game, against Nigeria, a dangerous, physically gifted team that put up three goals on Sweden. My mental demons are running amok as the game approaches. I feel as if I've let the team, myself, and James down. How could someone who a mere week ago was poised to have the tournament of her life suddenly turn into a missing-in-action midfielder?

Knowing I'm not in a good frame of mind, Hope invites me to join her and her husband, Jerramy, for lunch and a drive into the mountains. We ride on a gondola. The majesty of the Canadian Rockies is breathtaking. It takes me to a different mental place, turns off that endless self-critical loop for a while. Afterward we take in a lumberjack show, an attraction that I don't run across too often in South Jersey. There's axe-throwing and logrolling and crosscut sawing, beefy men in red flannel shirts everywhere you look. I'm not contemplating a career change, but it's cool to see people who are really into what they do.

Back down at sea level, the biggest challenge facing me isn't how I am playing. It is how I am thinking. I have almost no clarity. I am judging myself without mercy. I am in danger of wallowing my way right out of the World Cup. About the only thing I feel sure about is that if there is anyone who can help quiet the noise in my head, it is my trainer of twelve years.

James Galanis.

So we talk. James reminds me that Nigeria represents another opportunity for a fresh start.

"Start small when you go out there," he says. "Don't take big risks or play long through balls in the beginning. Keep it simple. Focus on having a clean touch and making a clean pass. Once you start to feel better and your confidence improves, then you start doing more involved things. The important thing is to create some success, build up a nice body of work over the first half, say, and let's see where we go from there."

On a designed play off the opening kickoff, I ping a fifty-yard ball on target to Abby's head, and it almost results in a goal in the first twenty seconds. It's as good a ball as I've played in three games, an encouraging way to start. James's plan seems to be working. I am easing into things, resisting the urge to do too much, taking better care of the ball, not fretting so much about making mistakes. In the fourteenth minute, I yank an open left-footed shot from distance way wide, not a good strike at all. But I don't get down on myself, and a few minutes later send a perfect twenty-yard ball on the ground up the middle for Alex to run onto.

Jill still has me deeper in the midfield than I'd prefer, but Holiday and I are a bit more involved. We're starting to combine on a few things offensively. I just miss converting a sliding chance off of a set piece by the left post late in the half, before Abby pounds in a corner kick in the forty-fifth minute to give us a lead. The half is far from a masterpiece, but it's the best we've played so far.

Keep playing simply. Let the game come to you, I tell myself at the half.

In the fifty-seventh minute, Pinoe has the ball on the right side and plays a nice square ball for me about five yards outside the box. I have space, and I am about to run onto it and bury it when the ball clips the referee's foot. It never reaches me. I fling up my arms in frustration and run back to defend.

I wonder what else could possibly go haywire in this tournament.

We advance to the knockout round with a 1–0 victory, but I can't escape the feeling that, even with a slight upgrade against Nigeria, my World Cup has been an abject disaster. The U.S. isn't advancing because of me but in spite of me.

Is that an overreaction? No doubt it is. The problem again is my level of expectation, my quest for perfection. It skews everything. When it flares up, it robs me of joy.

Jill reassures me again that it will be fine and that even top players go through these rough patches. The next day, she and Michelle French, an assistant coach, show me clips of the Nigeria game, highlighting opportunities I had to change the pace of things and play a greater variety of passes, the way I do when I am right. Switching fields and knocking accurate, long-range passes are two of my strengths. Now I am playing as if the ball is covered with poison ivy and I just want to get it away from me.

We fly to Edmonton to get ready to play Colombia five days later. Our hotel is near a shopping mall, and on an off day, James all but orders me to do some retail therapy.

"Don't train. Don't work out. Don't even think about soccer," James says. "Give yourself a break."

I hit Banana Republic and J. Crew and a few other stores,

picking up a few things. It's not as mind-clearing as the gondola and the lumberjacks, but at least I stop overanalyzing everything for a while. The day off is good. I go back to work and concentrate on all the basics — my first touches, the weight of my passes, and my shooting mechanics — and being aware of all the options that are out there for me on the field. Seeing those film clips with Jill and Frenchie helps. I need to get back to my attacking mentality.

I am tired of playing it safe.

IIIII

Do not underestimate the power of a single goal. Even a goal that comes from the penalty spot. In the sixty-sixth minute of our game against Colombia, we are holding a 1–0 lead in an unexpectedly tight game when Pinoe gets dragged down in the box. The whistle blows. The referee points to the spot, our second PK opportunity in seventeen minutes. Abby took the first one, after the Colombia keeper was red-carded for tripping Alex in the penalty area. She took it left-footed and knocked it wide.

Abby looks at me and nods. She is our number-one PK taker, and I am number two. I look back at her. Her message is clear: *This one is yours.*

"Are you sure?" I ask.

She nods again.

I step up and put the ball on the spot. I walk back a half-dozen steps or so and wait for the whistle. I typically prepare for a PK the night before, visualizing how I am going to approach it. Sometimes I might change it up if I see something in the keeper's positioning or her approach (sorry, I am not sharing any state secrets about the variables involved). More often I stick with my plan. This time, I calmly drill the ball in the right center of the net as the keeper dives the other way.

Up by two goals now, we should be in good shape, even if we are still not reminding anybody of FC Barcelona with our creative playmaking. While Colombia's midfielder, Yoreli Rincon, my friend and former teammate, shows brief flourishes of great skill, as do her teammates, we continue to lurch impatiently around the box, showing little ability to break down the defense with any consistency.

Even when Colombia has to play a man down after the red card, we are not able to generate a whole lot. Whether it's bad passes or poor decision making, our possession game isn't sharp, making us dependent on a great individual play to create something. Kling delivered just that to set up my PK.

About ten minutes later, it's my turn to try to make a play. I get the ball in the attacking third, take a couple of people on, then hit a curling, right-footed shot toward the right side of the goal. The Colombian keeper dives to her left and smothers it. I thought it had a chance and am bummed it didn't go in, but that's okay.

This is more like it, I think. *I'm starting to feel like myself.*

I can't tell you for sure, but I don't think I would have made that run if I hadn't scored on the PK. The goal doesn't just put me on the board literally; it helps set me free psychologically. I'm nowhere near where I want to be, but I am getting closer.

After the game as I board the bus for our hotel, there is finally a glimmer of a break in the storm clouds that have been hanging over my spirit for the whole World Cup.

It's happening slowly, but it's happening.

I am about to be unleashed, I think. *That PK is going to recharge me, uplift me. I am going to be a whole different player. You wait and see.*

I am named Player of the Match by the people on the FIFA Technical Committee. We're in the quarterfinals. I don't say it out loud to anyone, but as I look out the bus window at the big western Canadian sky, there's a single thought in my head, above all others:

I am back.

17

ADDITION BY SUBTRACTION

THE GOOD FEELING OVER OUR advancement into the final eight of the World Cup is tempered by the loss of two frontline players, Megan Rapinoe and Lauren Holiday. Both of them will miss our quarterfinal against China in Ottawa for exactly what Jill and her staff were worried about with me: yellow cards. Pinoe and Lauren got carded for a second time in the Colombia game, and even though I think both of the calls were borderline at best, rules are rules. So now we go into our biggest game of the tournament without two mainstays.

Two nights before the China game, Jill asks me to visit her in her room.

"I'm thinking of changing things up and moving you forward and giving you room to roam behind the forward line," she says. "We can have Morgan [Brian] sitting behind you. I'm not set on this yet, but I think it's a good way to go. China is very organized defensively, and I think we're going to need for you to be more of a presence in the attacking third."

Jill shows me clips of the Chinese defense, and we talk some more about my expanded role. I'm so happy, I could hug her. I want nothing more than to be a true attacking midfielder. For all the heat we've taken in this tournament — and the media is burying us, even after three victories and a tie — I know we have better soccer in us, and we're all ready to show it.

As if to prove it, I settle a ball in the second minute of our game and see Amy Rodriguez making a run toward the goal. I flick it ahead to her between two defenders. Amy is in alone, a quality chance right out of the chute, but with the keeper rushing at her, she shanks her shot wide.

Still, we send an early message to the Chinese, and we don't let up. We apply high pressure, and we keep possession when we win the ball. It doesn't result in immediate goals, but there's no question we are dominating play, particularly at the end of the half, when we string together nine or ten straight passes. We have the ball zipping around like a ball in a pinball machine. Anyone who is paying attention can see we are a different team, bringing an attack that wasn't there in the first four games.

The first half finishes scoreless, but I like what we are

doing and know we are going to keep the pressure on. Kelley O'Hara and I combine for a good chance in the opening minutes of the second, and soon after, Tobin Heath fights hard for a fifty-fifty ball near midfield and draws a foul in the process. Kling quickly takes the free kick, sliding it over to Julie, who is completely unmarked. Julie lifts a long ball into the box. I see it coming and make a run toward the goal. Though I am tightly marked, I believe if I anticipate correctly, I can get my head on the ball.

Julie's ball is perfect. I get a good read on it and jump up, heading the ball downward, knocking it past the Chinese goalkeeper. It takes until the fifty-first minute, but we are on the board. I run off to the corner to celebrate with a karate kick to the flag.

Two goals in two World Cup games? I'll take it.

China doesn't seriously threaten for the rest of the second half. For the first time in four games, we are connecting and creating, scoring a victory that is much more one-sided than the 1–0 score line would suggest. For the second consecutive game, I am named Player of the Match.

We move on to the semis to play Germany, which outlasted France in penalty kicks. Not many people give us much of a chance against Germany, two-time World Cup champions and the top-ranked team in the world. They have scored twenty goals and allowed only three in the tournament. (That's an impressive goal differential, even factoring in that the Germans scored ten of those goals in one game against Ivory Coast.) We're not concerned about who thinks what, though. We're concerned only with getting better.

||||

Almost from the start of our training together a dozen years ago, James would be in my ear constantly, with that thick Aussie accent of his.

"Don't let the coach take you off the field," he would say. "Play so it is not even an option. You want to get beyond politics and drama and all the nonsense? Just be better than everybody else. Give them no choice but to play you."

Now he is saying pretty much the same thing. When I tell him that Jill wants to keep me in the more forward position, even with Pinoe and Holiday back from their suspensions, he says, "Great. You know what the deal is. Play so she won't even consider moving you back to where you were."

So that is my goal as we travel to Montreal for the semis.

Once the Germans get by France, they are the popular pick to win the whole thing. Celia Sasic, their star striker, is the leading scorer in the tournament, with six goals. Her teammate Anja Mittag is right behind her with five. Their captain, Nadine Angerer, might be the best keeper in the world who is not named Hope Solo, and she proves it almost from the start, because after we absorb a few minutes of high-flying German pressure, we are in serious attack mode.

In the seventh minute, Julie runs onto a Pinoe corner kick, delivering a wicked header that Angerer makes a superb save on with her left foot. In the fourteenth minute, I slide a ball back to Tobin Heath, who threads it on the ground up the middle, a spectacular through ball that Alex runs onto. Alex one-times it, but again Angerer makes the stop with a left-footed block.

Already this game feels as if it's a heavyweight battle. The pace is furious, the intensity as real as the grass is phony. It is the best we've played in the entire tournament by far. We're combining well, moving the ball quickly, and making clever runs. Germany looks as if it has no idea how to handle us.

The half ends with no score, but we keep coming at them. We know Germany played 120 minutes against France, and we are the fresher team.

I have a good chance on a header off of another Pinoe corner kick in the opening minutes of the second half, but I don't get it on frame. Then in the fifty-sixth minute, I chip a ball to

Alex, and it looks as if it might be a breakaway before she gets tangled up with a defender and is called for a foul.

Germany has raised its level early in this half, and they are generating some threats. We just need to weather it and come back even stronger. In the fifty-ninth minute, Germany plays a seemingly harmless ball out of midfield that bounces toward our goal. Julie is in full retreat to clear it, but Germany's Alexandra Popp is running hard at goal and slips in front of Julie inside the box. She is about to get off a shot from point-blank range when Julie, in desperation, reaches for Popp's left shoulder and hauls her to the ground. The whistle blows. The referee points to the spot and gives Julie a yellow card. She actually got off light, because it easily could've been a red card for impeding the progress of a player going in on goal.

Julie has had a spectacular World Cup, but in this moment she is devastated by the opportunity she has given Germany to possibly steal the game. She starts to cry. Several players go over and put an arm around Julie to console her.

As Sasic steps forward to take the kick, Hope grabs her water bottle and goes for a leisurely stroll along the goal line. If there were flowers nearby, she would've stopped to pick them. She is out of the goal so long that she could've gotten a card herself. Hope is clearly aiming to get in Sasic's head, freeze her. At first Sasic looks as if she isn't sure she wants to take the kick. She seems to ask a few of her teammates if they want it. Hope finally returns to goal. Sasic puts her hands on her hips, looking very cavalier about the whole thing, then turns and claps her hands a few times. An instant before she starts her run-up, she turns her head to the side and smiles. Now she makes her approach and drives a low, hard ball to the left. Hope dives to the right.

Celia Sasic's ball veers just outside the left post.

The game is still tied. The crowd of some 51,000 people in Olympic Stadium lets out a collective roar. I let out my own roar.

Sometimes, even in the heat of a big game, you can feel the momentum shift on the spot. This is one of those times.

There is no way we are losing this game, I tell myself.

I turn to Julie.

"Keep your head up. Don't worry about it," I tell her. A couple of others make the same point.

A few minutes later, I can see that Julie is still moping, beating herself up.

"Cut it out, JJ. We have a game to win," I say.

About seven minutes after Sasic hits her ball wide left, I win control of a bouncing fifty-fifty ball and play it to Kling. She knocks it straight ahead to Alex, who has some space and is taking it. She's carrying the dribble near the top of the box when German defender Annike Krahn gets in her path and basically hip-checks her, sending Alex flying. By the time she lands, there is a whistle, a yellow card for Krahn, and a penalty kick for the United States.

It is mine to take. It's not clear if Krahn's contact with Alex is inside or outside the box. For sure, the initial bump is outside. I am not going to explore the matter with the ref. I walk straightaway to get the ball and put it on the spot. I have already visualized the PK the night before. I am going to go exactly where I went against Colombia. I step back from the ball and go to my shooting position. I am leaning forward, slightly bent at the waist, eyes fixed on the ball, nothing else. I don't look at the keeper or the crowd or anything else. Just the ball. I start my approach with a series of baby steps and then plant and kick, a clean, hard strike toward the upper right ninety. Angerer dives the opposite way. The ball rips into the net.

U.S. 1, Germany 0.

I take off running, clenching my fists, until my teammates catch up and mob me. I kiss my left ring finger and point to the television camera, my shout-out to Brian. Then it's back to business. There are twenty-one minutes plus stoppage time remaining. There's lots of work yet to do.

I want no part of bunkering and letting Germany seize

control of the game while we sit on our one-goal lead. I want to keep playing the way we have the whole game. In the seventy-sixth minute, I spin away from traffic, take a dribble, and nudge a ball out wide toward Kelley O'Hara. She has just come on for Tobin and is making a run down the right flank. It looks as if she might spring free before a German defender slide-tackles the threat away.

Kelley and I are not done, though. In the eighty-fourth minute, Holiday steps in and strips a German player near midfield and makes a run before knocking it out wide to the left, where Abby catches up and settles the ball, playing it back to Kling. Kling edges into the middle, takes two dribbles as I move away from her, and slips into an open space in the left side of the box. Kling carves a great pass to me. I take four quick dribbles, beat the defender out wide, and then cut a left-footed cross toward the middle but away from Angerer. Kelley sees this all developing and makes a perfectly timed run. She runs onto my cross and spears the ball with her right foot—into the goal.

It's her first international goal, and her timing is impeccable.

U.S. 2, Germany 0.

Still, there can't be any letup. Germany could answer

quickly and make it a one-goal game. Who knows what can happen? It's the final minutes of the sixth game of the World Cup, and I am going strong, powering up. I have James and Laurel Acres and years of fitness work to thank for that. In the ninetieth minute, the Germans are advancing the ball up the right side, and I make a thirty-yard sprint to apply pressure and disrupt it. Honestly, it's not a sprint I could have made in the first couple of games, when I was weighted down with discouragement. It's a sprint powered by belief. My energy supply feels inexhaustible. I go all out until the referee blows the whistle three times and points to midfield, and our whole bench rushes onto the field.

I am named Player of the Game for the third straight time, but the heroes are everywhere. Our back five completely shut down the most explosive offense at this tournament, and Kling, especially, was huge on her overlapping runs. Morgan Brian, at twenty-two the youngest player on the team, suffered what looked to be a nasty head injury in a violent first-half collision in the air with Alexandra Popp, but she was almost perfect otherwise. She kept possession and played with tremendous poise. Hope totally got into Sasic's head on the PK and made the saves she needed to.

We are bound for Vancouver, British Columbia, and the

World Cup final, a place few thought we would be even a week ago. I call James in Greece after the game.

"You're not done yet, Ms. Lloyd," he says. "You've trained for this moment for your whole life. This is no time to let up. Finish the job. Bring home the World Cup. Show the whole world the kind of player you are."

18

WORLD-BEATER

YOU KNOW HOW JAMES WOULD always tell me, "Play every game as if it's a World Cup final"? He doesn't have to say a thing on July 5, 2015, because I am in BC Place in Vancouver, and it is a World Cup final. The stadium is on the north side of False Creek, an inlet that separates downtown from the rest of the city. It has been inundated with true USA soccer fans who are hoping to see the first happy ending to a World Cup since 1999.

I have my own room for the final, on the twenty-fourth floor of the Sheraton Vancouver Wall Centre. Everything is great the night before, except that I keep waking up. I am thinking about the game, dreaming about the game. I don't visualize scoring five goals in the final, the way I did a few months earlier during a training session on Ark Road, but the game is in my head nonstop. I am so ready to play that my heart is racing, and I don't know how I am going to make it until the 5:00 p.m. kickoff.

I have so much energy, I don't know what to do with it. After breakfast I go for my fifteen-minute jog through downtown. Some people recognize me and wave and wish me good luck. I smile and wave back and keep going. I feel as though I could run for days. I organize everything in my room into tidy piles — the keepsakes and the Player of the Match frames and the clothes I bought on the James-ordered shopping trip.

One of our massage therapists stretches me out, and after a bite of lunch, I hydrate and stretch some more. Then I relax in the room with my headphones on. I've done most of my visualization the night before, but I get some more done throughout the day, not focusing on results so much as the process of playing the game . . . tackling hard, sending passes near and far, being strong in the attacking third.

Finally, it is almost time to leave for the game. I look down from my window and can see a big crowd of fans lining the barricaded walkway we'll take to our bus. There are hundreds of them, waiting to give us a proper sendoff.

The team meets in the lobby and then walks through a

gauntlet of rousing cheers and waving flags and choruses of the "I believe that we will win" chant that has swept through our fan base. I am filming it on my phone, smiling as I go. It is a very cool spectacle.

I board the bus and go to my spot, second row from the back on the right. Time to cue up "Dreamer" on my iPod again and reread James's final World Cup email. It is powerful and impassioned and uplifting, talking about how I am the best "Ms. Lloyd" I've ever been, because I have worked day after day as if I've achieved nothing, because I've stayed hungry and humble and done everything possible to be the best player I could be.

He signs off this way:

There will be no denying you if the underdog shows up again and owns this game. Go make this yours. You deserve it.

Signed,

The Planner

Reading over it again, I am filled with fresh gratitude for what my mentor/friend/trainer has done for me. James believed in me long before I did.

How do you thank somebody for that?

|||||

Jill sticks with the same lineup as the Germany game. I will be wearing the captain's armband again, along with my usual Nike Mercurial Vapor Super Fly boots, with the words FIVE PILLARS — the emblem of the University Soccer Academy — written on the side of each.

Jill huddles us up before we take the BC Place field. One of her best qualities as a coach is how straightforward she is. We're grown women, and we know what's in front of us. Jill honors that. She says simply, "We started this journey to get to this very point. You know what you need to do. There isn't much else to say. We are ready. Let's bring this trophy back home. Go out there, have fun, and enjoy it."

An explosion of noise greets us when we take the field, more than 50,000 people rocking the place. The sky is a smoky gray, and I mean literally smoky: wildfires are burning in the mountains outside the city, and by later that night, it will get so bad that there will be an environmental alert.

I take my spot along the center circle, at the half-field line, in the shaded half of the pitch. Seconds away now. Adrenaline is coursing through my body at Daytona 500 speed.

Japan, the defending champion, kicks off, but Lauren Holiday wins possession of a bouncing ball almost immediately and chips it out wide to me. I get my first touch eleven seconds into the game. I take three dribbles, make a cut, and play it up to Alex, who knocks it out wide to Ali Krieger, who hits Tobin Heath, who centers it back to Alex. Alex's left-footed touch is a bit heavy, but we connect five passes and are attacking not even thirty seconds into the game. I love it. We keep the combinations coming.

On our next foray into the Japanese end, Pinoe gets a pass from Kling and sends it crossfield to Morgan Brian. Morgan plays it to Ali and makes a run, and Ali slips for a second but scrambles to her feet and finds her. Morgan carries the ball toward the goal line and lets fly with a cross that is blocked, drawing a corner kick.

It is the third minute. Pinoe lines up to take the corner. Tony's design has a cluster of players in front, hoping for a head ball to play, and several others spread around the box. I am about thirty yards out, seemingly a complete bystander. As Pinoe begins her approach to take the kick, I sprint into the box on a bit of a diagonal run. Pinoe's kick is well struck and rolls quickly into the box, untouched. The play is built 100 percent on timing. If the kick is too slow or too fast, if I am too early or too late, it will go for nothing. Pinoe's corner is perfect. I run onto the ball and intersect with it just a stride inside the penalty spot. My focus is entirely on the ball, nothing else. I make contact with it using the outside of my left foot, and with the ball's pace and my pace, I do not have to strike it hard. The ball fires off my foot, a spinning rocket toward the left side of the Japanese goal. Keeper Ayumi Kaihori dives but has no chance. The ball blasts into the net, and after a momentary fall, I bound right back up and keep on running. I head to the corner, fists pumping and celebrating in front of the American Outlaws, U.S. soccer's unofficial fan club, and then hugging Pinoe and everybody else near the corner flag.

You could not ask for a better way to start.

It is not just one of our best goals of the whole tournament; it is one of the best goals of the year — not because I score it but because the execution on everybody's part, especially Pinoe's corner and the player movements that opened up the space, is perfect. The Japanese players look as if they've just been hit by a tractor-trailer.

The tractor-trailer is not stopping.

Tobin makes a great run down the right side and gets taken down just outside the box, and we have another set piece in the fifth minute. Holiday takes this one and drives it low and hard to Julie Johnston, who has edged toward the near post. I am at the 18-yard line and make a run as soon as Lauren makes contact. Julie's job is to get a piece of the ball and send it on behind her, into the middle, and she does it beautifully. The ball caroms toward the front of the goal, glances off a Japanese player's hand, and here I come, unmarked at first, crashing the goal, then beating two defenders to the ball and using the inside of my foot to put it past Kaihori to make it 2–0. BC Place is quaking, it is so loud, and again I just keep on running, putting my arm around Lauren and then leading our whole team on a sprint across the field, all the way to the bench, where we have a spontaneous group hug.

Who can even believe this is happening? It is the greatest start to a World Cup game the U.S. has ever had, the greatest start to a game that I have ever had.

It is almost an out-of-body experience, the way this game has begun. Japan tries to settle itself and create the possession it is so good at, but Becky Sauerbrunn, a rock in the back during the whole World Cup, intercepts a pass and plays it up to Morgan Brian. Morgan directs it out wide to Tobin. Tobin takes a few touches and chips a long ball into the box, toward Alex, but a missed clearance leaves the ball bouncing inside the box. Holiday takes full advantage, stepping up and volleying it, a superb strike that blows right past Kaihori, who must have no idea what has hit her.

We are in the fourteenth minute and we are up 3–0, and the rollicking fans are just cheering nonstop. The Japanese team huddles up before the kickoff, trying somehow to stay composed and probably reminding themselves they have more than seventy-five minutes to even the score. It doesn't help.

They connect ten passes on their next possession, but near the half-field circle, I intercept a bad backpass and take a touch, eluding a Japanese player and starting upfield. I take a second touch and look up to see who is open and how best to attack, when I notice that Kaihori is off her line — way off her line — near the 18. I know if I hit it right, I can get the ball over her and put it on goal.

I have been practicing these midfield shots since my Medford Strikers days.

It's worth a shot, I tell myself.

Maybe a foot inside the center line, fifty-four yards from the Japanese goal, I push the ball far enough in front of me that I can take a full swing at it. I power up to the ball and drive it toward the goal. Kaihori sees what I am doing and begins a desperate retreat. My ball has just the right trajectory, high enough to carry but low enough that Kaihori doesn't have much time to recover. She keeps retreating, and it doesn't make it any easier that I am shooting from the shadows and she is looking straight into the sun. She stumbles backwards at about the 6-yard line, and as she falls, she manages to get her right hand on the ball, slightly redirecting it.

It is not enough.

The ball bounces once, ticks off the left post, and goes

into the net, with Ayumi Kaihori sprawled on her back right in front of it.

We have entered the realm of the surreal. Japan gave up two goals in six previous games. And now we have scored four in sixteen minutes. Are you kidding? I am running and laughing, holding two index fingers aloft, trying to comprehend what is happening but knowing there is no chance. Hope almost never comes out of goal to celebrate, but she runs up to join us this time.

She hugs me and says, "Are you even human?"

I don't know what I am. I just know we are up 4–0 on a great team, sixteen minutes into the World Cup final, and we aren't letting up. It's barely two minutes later when Pinoe chips a sweet ball to Kling, who arches a perfect little cross in front. I go up and put a head on it, knocking it toward the near post, but just wide.

It might be the easiest chance I have had all day.

The Japanese break through in the twenty-seventh minute on a goal by forward Yuki Ogimi, who spins in the box and curls a beautiful shot into the upper left corner. They pick up their level at the end of the half, and Jill warns us at the break not to get complacent and sit back. We need to keep up the pressure and the attacking mentality that got us the lead.

Just five minutes into the second half, Japanese midfielder Aya Miyama takes a long free kick, which skims off Julie's head into the corner of the goal. Japan has cut our lead in half, and if we learned anything in the Cup final four years earlier, when Japan twice came back from one-goal deficits, this is not a team that goes away.

You can tell they are starting to believe they can do this, and there's still almost forty minutes to play. We need to answer. On our ensuing possession, we put pressure on the Japanese back line. I control a loose ball near the top of the box, carry it in, and push it ahead to Alex. She is rebuffed, but we keep possession, and soon Kling and Alex work a nice give-and-go that leads to a corner kick. Holiday lofts it right in front of the goal. Kaihori tries to punch it away but muffs the clearance, and the ball goes beyond her to Morgan Brian, who centers it to Tobin, who is unmarked in front and pounds it in.

The lead is back to three, and we are not letting up. I win a ball in the middle third and make my longest run of the day deep into the attacking third before hitting Pinoe on the left side of the box. I nearly take advantage of sloppy Japanese defense and almost beat Kaihori to a backpass before she grabs it. Kelley O'Hara, who comes on for Pinoe, continues her dynamic play and has two good chances right away.

The game moves beyond the seventieth minute, and Japan is playing some of its best soccer of the game. Hope makes a fine clearance on a high ball, and the defense stays tight and organized, giving the supremely skilled Japanese little room to create.

In the seventy-ninth minute, the greatest goal-scorer in the history of international soccer, Abby Wambach, comes on for Tobin. A huge ovation resounds through BC Place. I go over to the sideline, take off the captain's armband, and strap it on Abby. This will be the final World Cup game of her career. It's only right that she goes out with the armband.

The clock keeps moving, but I am oblivious to it. Even as I see our bench and coaching staff standing arm in arm, I am fighting for loose balls, trying to keep possession. Now we move into stoppage time, one minute and then another and then a third, and I am chasing a ball that sails over my head when the three whistles blow and the stadium erupts one more time.

I drop to my knees and am almost instantly overcome by emotion. I don't cry in public, ever. I guess I make an exception when we win a World Cup. The coaches and the whole team pour onto the field, running so fast you'd think they were being chased. Heather O'Reilly is the first to reach me. She bends down and wraps her arms around me, and there we are in BC Place by False Creek, two Jersey girls reveling in the happy, smoky moment. Other players also head to the edge of the field to find their family and friends and drink in the love. I don't go over to the stands, because I don't think anybody is there. Soon enough, I find out I am wrong: Aunt Patti, my cousins Jaime and Adam, and my best friend Karen all secretly made the trip for the final. Brian thought hard about it, but in the end wanted to respect my wishes.

My parents? They are not here. I don't even know if they watched. I never hear a word until my mother sends a card a few weeks later.

After the medal ceremony, and after I receive the Golden Ball for being the Player of the Tournament, I return to the locker room and can't find my phone at first, because it's somewhere beneath all the layers of cellophane they've covered the locker room with to protect our stuff from spraying champagne. When I finally dig it out, there are more than 400 text messages. I call Brian first, and it's so wonderful to hear the joy in his voice.

"I am so happy and proud of you," Brian says.

"I can't wait to celebrate with you," I say.

When I reach James, he says, "What's going on?"

"Not much," I say. "Just won a World Cup and scored some goals."

"I told you you could do it," he says.

"I know. And I am not stopping now. When are we training next? I want to keep getting better."

James stops me. "Ms. Lloyd, relax and enjoy the moment. We will train soon enough."

I meet up with Aunt Patti, Jaime, Adam, and Karen.

I hug them all and tell them, "I can't believe you are here!" Jaime and Karen stay with me in my room that night, even though I never go to bed. I am way too excited and way too happy to sleep. The team party goes loud and late. For once I am not in my room, hydrating and stretching. I am in the middle of everything. It's the best sleepless night of my life.

19

PURE GOLD

ONE HUNDRED NINETY-ONE DAYS after our triumph over Japan and what people are calling the greatest performance in the history of the World Cup finals, I have traded in my white number 10 USA uniform and Nike boots for a red Matthew Christopher gown and high heels. I am with Brian, sitting directly behind Ronaldo in the second row of a huge auditorium in a swanky building called Kongresshaus, on the shores of Lake Zurich in Switzerland.

The event is FIFA's annual gala, Ballon d'Or (French for "Gold Ball"). The date is January 11, 2016. I have played soccer all over the world, but I've never been to Zurich until now. I am here because I am a finalist for the most prestigious award a soccer player can receive—FIFA's World Player of the Year. The greatest players in the sport are all around me, among them Lionel Messi, Neymar, and my personal favorite, Andres Iniesta, the incomparable midfielder for FC Barcelona. On the women's side, the notables include my fellow finalists, Aya Miyama of Japan and Celia Sasic of Germany, the star players of our last two opponents in the World Cup, along with my friend and teammate Hope Solo, who is on the shortlist for Player of the Year honors as well.

I am accompanied by my three allotted guests: Brian, James, and James's older son, Astin. The room is very warm, and between that and my nerves—I am more nervous by far than I've ever been for an Olympic or World Cup final—my hands and feet are slick with sweat. I've been nervous ever since I arrived in Switzerland, almost unable to eat, sleeping fitfully, my fuel mostly consisting of cappuccinos. Brian and I are holding hands, but I keep having to pull away to dry myself off a bit. When you play, you can work out the nerves by running for a ball or tackling somebody. At Ballon d'Or, there is nothing to do but sit and wait and hope your name is called, kind of like FIFA's version of the Oscars.

Between the time the master of ceremonies says, "I proudly present the FIFA Women's World Player of the Year," and opens the envelope, it feels as if a full ninety minutes goes by, plus ten minutes of stoppage time. I think my heart might pound right out of my gown. It keeps pounding until I hear the emcee say:

"Carli Lloyd."

I want to get up and run around as if I am celebrating a goal, but I play it cool instead. The happiness I feel is almost indescribable. I give Brian a kiss and begin the walk up onto the stage. I successfully make the trip without a tumble and gratefully receive the trophy, which is so heavy I could do curls with it.

"Wow," I say.

I am overcome in the moment and take four or five seconds to collect myself. I apologize, and the crowd applauds. Finally, I think I'm calm enough to get through my remarks, which I've been thinking about for a couple of days.

Here's what I say:

"It truly is an honor. This has been a dream of mine ever since I started my journey with the national team.

"Celia . . . Aya . . . [You are] phenomenal footballers just as deserving of this award.

"I want to thank everyone who voted for me. Also I want to thank Sunil Gulati and everyone at U.S. Soccer for all their support. I also want to thank Jill [Ellis] and the coaching staff [and] all of our support staff. I honestly wouldn't be sitting up here — standing up here — without my incredible teammates, and we all know it took twenty-three players to win the World Cup this past summer, so thank you to them.

"To my friends and family at home, thank you for your

support. To my fiancé, Brian, I couldn't have done this without your support. I love you. To James, we started this journey thirteen years ago. You told me that I could become the best player in the world. It just took me the realization now that I could. Thank you for everything. One last shout-out: Astin Galanis, Preston Galanis, keep working hard. Keep your dreams and just go after 'em.

"Thank you, everybody."

The whole night is a blur. It gets even better when Jill Ellis, who took over our team just a little more than a year out from the World Cup, is named the Women's Coach of the Year. Afterward, I pose for photos with Messi, the men's Ballon d'Or winner, and get to meet Ronaldo, Marcelo, Kaka, and a who's who of other world-class players. I even sneak in a quick photo with Iniesta.

The gala dinner is in the room next door, but even then I barely eat because I am too excited and people keep coming by and wanting photos. It is a blast, but by now I really want out of the gown and heels.

The next day I fly home. During the flight, I order a cheeseburger and fries — a meal I have maybe once a year — and try to comprehend everything that has happened in the last twenty-four hours.

Am I really returning home from the Ballon d'Or? Did I

really hear my name called out before the greatest players in the world, after being voted FIFA's Women's World Player of the Year?

When you work toward a goal for this long, you can't even fathom how you might feel once you achieve it. I still cannot fathom it now, and in some ways I am not sure I even want to, because I do not want to stop here. I want to keep getting better and better. I don't want to be satisfied, ever. That may sound grim, but it isn't at all. It is joyful, because the pursuit of progress is joyful. Playing the game I love is joyful.

So I keep pushing, keep working.

I am, after all, a soccer player. Give me a ball and let's go.

"When you are on the field, you aren't competing against anybody," James says. "You are competing against yourself. The competition is who you were yesterday and your goal is to be better than that today. Your opponent on match day is not another team; it's your previous performance."

Not every performance will be better than the one before, of course. The first three games of the World Cup were a painful reminder of that. The point is that if you are not driven to improve, the only possible options are staying the same or getting worse, neither of which is acceptable.

It seems as if it were decades ago now, but once I wanted to quit soccer. My U-21 coach, Chris Petrucelli, sent me packing from the national team, telling me that I wasn't good enough and didn't work hard enough. For a time I was ready to accept his assessment and go find a job that didn't involve cleats and shin guards, but then my father connected me with a man named James Galanis, and everything changed.

James offered me so much more than deep soccer expertise. He offered hope. He offered belief. He offered a commitment of time and energy that was beyond all measure — truly 24/7, 365 days a year.

It seems like pure fantasy, doesn't it? A little-known trainer in South Jersey is going to take on a U-21 reject and make her the world's best player? Right. And for his next trick, he will swim to Australia and back.

More than a few people thought James was completely grandiose, a charlatan, or both. They thought I was a misguided minion who had fallen under his spell. Nobody believed. Even James's wife, Colleen, had her doubts. What very few ever understood was how hard we worked all year round, at all hours of the night and day. It would've been easy to cut corners, but we never did, because we knew we couldn't, and that is how we are doing things even now.

So there we are under the dim lights on Ark Road, working on side volleys in the cold and damp of December. There we are, refining first touches and crosses in the heat and humidity of July. There we are in the Blue Barn in winter, or in Laurel Acres whenever, James devising the workout plans and me punishing my body according to his specifications. There are scores of world-class players, maybe hundreds of them, who are deeply committed to their work and train incredibly hard. I would never say that I outwork all of them, because how could I really know that?

All I can tell you is that for thirteen years James Galanis and I, mentor and pupil, have poured every ounce of our energy and passion into this mad-scientist project of his.

Whatever else you want to say, it's worked out pretty well.

James secretly loved that nobody believed in us, and he taught me to love it. He relished it when I was benched or criticized or overlooked, when other U.S. players were commanding the spotlight, because he knew it would be gasoline for my internal fire. What can I tell you?

I thrive on that Jersey edge.

I love to prove people wrong.

Now that my teammates and I are World Cup champions and I've been named FIFA's Women's World Player of the Year, I'm not sure how I will continue to be an underdog. But trust me, I will find a way. Somebody will write that it was a fluke, or that I am over the hill, or that I just got really lucky in those opening sixteen minutes against Japan. Or maybe it will be something else. Whatever it is, I will find someone to prove wrong and then work my butt off to do just that.

I can't tell you that the path I've taken has been easy. It has been filled with doubts and despair, tears and trauma, with a difficult family situation that I still hope can be mended. I've said it before and will say it again: without my parents, none of this — the World Cup and Olympic titles, my career, to say nothing of this book — would've been possible.

I don't know all the answers, or even half of them. I just know what works for me. So what do I want to leave you with? Listen to your heart and try always to do the right thing. Put everything you have into your passions, because one of the greatest gifts in life is to be able to do what you love. Cherish the people who love and support you unconditionally, for they are life's greatest treasure.

Life is complicated. Life is going to throw all kinds of obstacles in your way. All I can tell you is what works for me: be true to yourself, don't do fake, and above all else, keep on working, because that's what will take you where you want to go.

EPILOGUE

IN THE SUMMER OF 2016, I headed down to Rio with my U.S. teammates determined to help the U.S. become the first country to capture an Olympic gold medal the year after winning a World Cup. I had spent the first part of the summer rehabbing a sprained knee, but I felt fitter and strong than ever. I was completely confident that we would fulfill our mission.

Unfortunately, it didn't quite work out that way.

Instead of coming home with a third Olympic gold, I boarded the flight back to Jersey with nothing but disappointment. We lost to Sweden in the quarterfinals on penalty kicks, making it the first time the U.S. did not win a medal.

As a co-captain and team leader, I took the result especially hard. But as I reflect on it now, the result is only making me more motivated to empty the tank and do everything I can to help us get back on top. To me, that's the best and healthiest way to respond to a setback. Indeed, it is the only way to respond. You can't go back and change what happened. All you can do is shift your focus and energy to a place where it can do you some good. It's easier said than done, of course, but if you ask me it's the only option. You never give in. You never give up. You go after your goals with full effort — and pure heart. It's the best way I know to get everything you want out of life.

ACKNOWLEDGMENTS

I'VE KNOWN FOR A LONG time that it takes eleven players to make a strong soccer team. I've learned that it takes many more players than that to make for a successful book.

Josh Weil and Jay Mandel at William Morris Entertainment set this project in motion, connecting me with a top-notch publisher in Houghton Mifflin Harcourt and a wonderful editor in Susan Canavan. Susan believed in the project and its message from the outset, and so did the whole world-class team at HMH: Bruce Nichols, Jenny Xu, Martha Kennedy, Megan Wilson, and Hannah Harlow.

I want to thank everyone at U.S. Soccer. The senior officials, coaches, medical staff, trainers, massage therapists, equipment managers, and support staff—all of you are consummate pros and have played a huge role in supporting and helping me throughout my career.

I am lucky to have the support of such great sponsors as

Nike, NJM Insurance Company, Hand and Stone, and Comcast; thank you for believing in me.

So many people in the Delran community have encouraged me from the time I started playing. I can't begin to name them all, but Delran is where my journey began and you were all a huge part of it.

Rudi Klobach, late coach of Delran High School, led our team to two state championship games and was as passionate about soccer as anyone I've ever met. All of my teammates at Delran High were a part of memories that will stay with me forever. The late Joe Dadura, founder and inspiration of the Medford Strikers, provided me with six of the best years of my soccer life and with friendships that have lasted even longer. To Kacy, Maureen, Venice, and Quinn—PITA will never forget you, or the Original 5. To all of my Strikers teammates, thank you for making every practice and every game so much fun.

My thanks to my Rutgers coach, Glenn Crooks, for giving the great gift of allowing me to play with freedom and creativity—to express myself on the field. I was fortunate to have such wonderful teammates and roommates as Tara Froelich and Christine Wentzler and so many other tremendous Scarlet Knights over four years.

Jerry Smith gave me a chance with the U-21s, and I have

never forgotten that. Chris Petrucelli gave me honesty that changed my life. Jill Ellis was a wonderful coach with the U-21s, and I have enjoyed continuing this journey with her; thank you for your respect and belief in me, Jill.

For years the people of Evesham Township, New Jersey, have generously allowed me the use of the Blue Barn to train in. Without the Blue Barn, this story never would've happened.

The students and staff of Universal Soccer Academy have been my soccer soulmates forever. Thank you for helping me become a better player and human being.

There's nothing more special than friendship. Thanks to Heather Mitts, my longtime teammate and training buddy, who understood and befriended me from the start. You have always been there for me and helped me along the way. Thank you. Hope Solo is not only a world-class goalkeeper, she has been a dear friend to me on this unforgettable journey. Thank you for always believing in me and being there for me.

John Johnson, my attorney, has always looked after me and protected me. You have been such an important piece of my success, and I can't thank you enough. You are the best lawyer anyone could have. Karen and Kathy Sweet are twin sisters and twin best friends, and I cannot tell you how much I cherish you both for your amazing love and friendship.

To my in-laws, Kathy Hollins; Bob Hollins; Lisa, Jim, Tyler, and Kyle Gonteski; Lucy Ebert; Debbie Teisman; Ann Marie and Amanda Holloway; Ed, Joe, and Chris Ebert—thank you for all your kindness and support. I'm so happy that we are all officially family.

To Colleen, Astin, and Preston Galanis, you have all become my extended family, and I can't thank you enough for all your support. I love you guys.

Jaime Bula, my cousin, was my idol growing up and is now my biggest supporter. Thank you for always being there for me.

Aunt Patti, Aunt Sandy, and Uncle Wayne—you have always been there for me, in good times and bad. The support you have provided me throughout my life has been priceless, and I can't thank you enough. Uncle Phil—I miss you and will never forget the time you gave me a bloody nose. You toughened me up! You were always my number-one fan—I know you are celebrating my journey from above. To my grandfather, Pop-pop, I miss you and Grandmom Carol: Thank you for all our fun times and visits together. I will forever cherish those moments. To my cousins—Adam Wilson, Brent Carr, Kerrie DaVanon, Bryan and Craig Wilson—you are the best, and I hope you know that.

The Bula, DaVanon, Jackson, Carr, and Fornaro families have long been a major part of my life. I love you all.

To James's mom, Vicky, thanks so much for all of your support—all the way from Down Under.

My co-author, Wayne Coffey, showed amazing dedication throughout the writing process and pushed and prodded me to make the message of this book authentic and empowering. I cannot thank him enough for the countless hours he put in to tell my story.

Thank you to my parents for your support and encouragement throughout my younger years as a soccer player. Your dedication and commitment to helping me follow my dreams is very much appreciated. I will never forget the times I shared with you, both on the soccer field and at home. Without you, I would not be who I am today. To my sister, Ashley, and brother, Stephen, I thank you for everything you have done for me. We had great times together growing up, and I will forever cherish these moments.

Brian Hollins, you are my love, my everything. You are the most patient man on earth. I can't thank you enough for all the support you have given me throughout my journey. None of this would have been possible without your love. I love you more than anything, Brian.

James Galanis has so many roles in my life, I am not sure where to start. He is a professor, a trainer, a mentor, a friend. He saved my career, believed in me when no one else did, set a goal and never wavered from working hard each and every day to make it happen. It took me thirteen years to realize that I could become the best player in the world. He taught me how to become strong and conquer anything that comes my way.

I can try to thank you for all that you've done for me as a player and person, James, but words would never be enough. I guess they'll have to do, though, won't they, mate?

AUTHOR'S NOTE

TO MY READERS:

I did not write the book you are holding to get rich, or for the thrill of seeing my name and picture on the cover. I wrote it because I wanted to share my journey with you.

Every single one of us faces challenges and adversity in our lives. Winning a World Cup doesn't give you immunity from that. I have dealt with rejection, defeat, and insecurities. I've lived with doubts and fears that felt overwhelming at times. But I have learned that just because you have these feelings doesn't mean they have to stop you. No, life is not always easy. Things don't always go the way we want them to. If you take nothing else from this book, please know that if you stay positive and give everything you've got, you can overcome whatever obstacles might be in front of you.

I can just about guarantee that you will run into people who will be negative and will tell you that you've got no shot at going where you dream of going. You know what you should do with such people? Ignore every single word they say. Avoid them as if they were a virus.

Whether your goal is to play for the U.S. Women's National Team, go to medical school, or work with underprivileged people, the only way to get there, as I like to say, is to "empty the tank" every day. That's exactly what I have done. It's what I continue to do. If you believe in yourself and truly commit to doing your best in everything you do, there's no telling where *your* journey will take you